THE TRADE CARD
IN NINETEENTH-CENTURY AMERICA

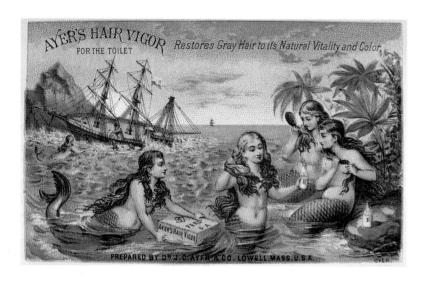

ROBERT JAY

THE TRADE CARD
IN NINETEENTH-CENTURY AMERICA

UNIVERSITY OF MISSOURI PRESS
COLUMBIA, 1987

Copyright © 1987 by
The Curators of the University of Missouri
University of Missouri Press, Columbia, Missouri 65211
Printed and bound in the United States of America

Library of Congress Cataloging-in-Publication Data

Jay, Robert.
    The trade card in nineteenth-century America.

    Bibliography: p.
    Includes index.
    1. Advertising cards—United States—History—
19th century.   I. Title.   II. Title: Trade card in
19th-century America.
HF5851.J39   1987   769.5   86-30902
ISBN 0-8262-0619-0 (alk. paper)

∞™ This paper meets the minimum requirements of
the American National Standard for Permanence of Paper
for Printed Library Materials, Z39.48, 1984.

The illustration on p. *ii* is from the author's collection.
The illustration on p. *vi* is used courtesy of The Warshaw
Collection of Business Americana, Smithsonian Institution.
The illustration on p. *viii* is used courtesy of Rare Books
and Manuscripts Division, The New York Public Library.
Astor, Lenox and Tilden Foundations.

TO MY PARENTS

ACKNOWLEDGMENTS

I am grateful to the institutions that assisted me by providing reproductions of trade cards in their collections and by giving me access to their collections. Special thanks go to the following individuals: Georgia Bumgardner, of the American Antiquarian Society; Lorene B. Mayo, of the Smithsonian Institution; and Helena Zinkham, of The New-York Historical Society, who provided many substantial suggestions regarding early trade cards. I want to thank Amy Oshiro for unstinting help in the preparation of the manuscript.

My friend Richard R. Taylor also deserves special thanks. Rick's broad-ranging interests in American popular culture, and in trade cards in particular, did much to inspire my own interest in this subject.

Credits for illustrations are given in the individual captions. On all dimensions, measurement of height (vertical) precedes breadth (horizontal). Measurements are in inches.

Young Columbus.

CONTENTS

Acknowledgments, v

Introduction, 1

CHAPTER ONE

The Trade Card
in the Seventeenth and
Eighteenth Centuries, 4

CHAPTER TWO

The Evolution
of the American Trade Card
in the Nineteenth Century, 13

CHAPTER THREE

The Advertiser
and the Trade Card, 34

CHAPTER FOUR

The Major Themes, 61

EPILOGUE

The Demise
of the Trade Card, 99

Notes, 104

Bibliography, 107

Index, 111

In the broadest sense of the term, advertising is as old as civilization itself. Ancient craftsmen signed their wares in hopes of future sales; in Roman cities, merchants hung signs outside their shops to attract prospective customers. However, advertising in the form of printed circulars or announcements is a relatively recent phenomenon in Western civilization. The technical means, specifically the media of printing, had already existed for about three centuries before any significant printed advertising developed; it was the actual need for such advertising that was slow to develop. The practice of printing quantities of cards or sheets to advertise the offerings of specific tradesmen began only late in the seventeenth century, and was at first primarily an urban phenomenon. Advertising by means of the engraved tradesman's card was especially popular in London and other commercially competitive British cities. From the time that the medium first emerged around 1700, trade cards were usually illustrated, relying on visual appeal and wit to attract the attention of the customer. Like the tradesmen themselves, such cards soon appeared in the American colonies as well, where they served to publicize the rapidly growing trades of Boston and other cities. The style of illustration and the letter design of American trade cards from the colonial period were most commonly modeled after examples that had come from England. Generally, cards printed in this period advertised luxury goods produced by skilled craftsmen, and thus were intended primarily for a

sophisticated and literate audience. The range of items advertised may have been small, but these richly illustrated examples of early American printing nonetheless tell us a good deal about the rapid growth of commerce and the skilled crafts in eighteenth-century America. For this reason alone, the trade cards of colonial America undoubtedly deserve the same kind of devoted study that Ambrose Heal so expertly made of eighteenth-century English examples.

Although this book briefly examines the eighteenth-century background, it is concerned primarily with American trade cards of the nineteenth century. This is partly because the material from this period survives in so much greater quantity. In nineteenth-century America, the illustrated trade card developed more rapidly, and was adapted to a greater variety of uses, than anywhere else in the industrialized world. The uniquely American exploitation of this medium is evident from the beginning of the century, when American printers began to develop their own approaches to imagery, approaches that no longer relied on the British influences of the colonial period. Although the actual printing of trade cards was at first limited primarily to the urban centers of Boston, New York, and Philadelphia, engravers in smaller towns also began to produce illustrated cards for their business clients as the population and industry of the country expanded. However, it was not until the introduction of the technology of lithography that trade cards became readily accessible to businesses and

manufactures throughout the United States. From the time of its arrival in America in the 1820s, lithography rapidly displaced engraving as a commercial printing medium. Lithography was relatively lower in cost and could provide an almost limitless number of prints from a single prepared stone. It was also much more flexible in terms of the ease of preparing the plate and the larger dimensions that were possible. From the standpoint of the public interest in trade cards, by far the most important development was lithographic printing in several colors, which began to appear in the manufacture of some cards in the 1860s. The key figure in the shift to full-color printing of trade cards was Louis Prang, who in the 1870s developed the idea of mass-producing small cards that could be adapted to the needs of individual advertisers at very low cost. Prang was soon followed in this field by a number of large-scale lithographic printers in eastern cities. By the time of the Centennial Exhibition held in Philadelphia in 1876, all the elements were in place for a dramatic expansion in the use of the trade card, to the point where it became a pervasive, even ubiquitous advertising medium in the United States. During the 1880s and the 1890s, illustrated trade cards would reach the height of their popularity, not only with the advertisers themselves, but also with the American public, which became remarkably interested in collecting them.

Mass-produced trade cards were common in several industrialized countries in the later years of the nineteenth century, but nowhere were they used to advertise such a wide variety of products, and nowhere did they provide such a comprehensive view of contemporary society, as in the United States. To fully understand the unique value of trade cards as a reflection of American social history in this period, one must consider the enormous industrial and commercial growth, as well as the sheer increase in population, that characterized the last third of the century. The population of the United States almost doubled between 1870 and 1900, and yet during this period industrial and agricultural production still outstripped consumption. From the early 1870s until the late 1890s, exports exceeded imports in all but three years. This favorable balance of trade was due in large part to the tremendous volume of American agricultural exports. Reaching a peak of almost 85 percent of exports in 1880, agricultural products still accounted for about 70 percent of foreign trade at the end of the century. In total production of manufactured goods, the United States went from fourth among industrialized nations in 1860 to first in 1894, producing as much as Great Britain, France, and Germany combined. Aided by a highly protective tariff system and a steady supply of cheap labor, industrialists were able to sell roughly 90 percent of their products at home, and at prices that progressively dropped as the century drew to a close. This situation, combined with the rapid increase in the American population, created a consumer market previously unparalleled in the Western world.

For both good and ill, the railroad system had an enormous impact on the American economy in the later nineteenth century. In 1865, there were just over three thousand miles of railroad west of the Mississippi River. By 1890, that amount had increased to over seventy-two thousand miles. Instrumental in the populating of the West, the railroads were perhaps even more important as the means of transporting the raw materials and agricultural products of the West to eastern port cities. As the population of the West slowly grew, railroads also became increasingly important in providing that region with the manufactured products that were flowing out of eastern factories. Perhaps more than any other factor, the extensive railroad system of the United States permitted the development of what would strike the English economist Alfred Marshall as "the homogeneity of the American demand for manufactured goods."[1] With markets in the Mid and Far West so easily accessible by railroad, it is little wonder that American industrialists placed so little emphasis on foreign exports compared to their European counterparts. However, the overwhelming importance of the railroads at times had distinctively unfortunate repercussions as well. Excessive speculation and expansion in the railroad industry, along with several instances of gross mismanagement, played a major role in bringing on a deep depression between 1873 and 1878, a second between 1883 and 1885, and a third lasting from 1893 to 1895. Thus, while the railroads were essential to the industrial and commercial expansion of the United States in the later nineteenth century, their negative impact in overly speculative conditions indicates just how unpredictable and even precarious the American economy was during much of this period.[2]

Along with dynamic industrialization and a rapid growth of its domestic market, later nineteenth-century America was characterized by a remarkable inventiveness in the development of new consumer products. The devout belief in a unique Yankee ingenuity had long since been ingrained in America's self-image, and was indeed considered inseparable from the spirit of republican freedoms bequeathed by the Revolution. In reference to the Centennial Exhibition of 1876, an editorialist for the *Nation* summarized the implications of this belief quite succinctly:

But if I were asked to name the potent factors of our ingenuity, I should find them in the early history of this country and in the form of government which was developed out of it. We live in what is emphatically the New World, and nothing of the Old that we wanted to shake off could cling to us. For having to depend upon ourselves we arrived at a state in which anything short of self-government was intolerable. Innovation became a sign of liberty, as it was really the fruit of liberty; it is now as natural for us to experiment as it is to breathe. Our mechanical superiority is therefore, it seems to me, the outgrowth of a moral principle for which we may take credit to ourselves; and as it has largely contributed to our material prosperity, perhaps this prosperity is too often, by foreigners, decried as purely material. No doubt it has changed self-reliance into overweening confidence in ourselves, has increased our contempt of precedents and our ignorance of what experience has taught other nations, especially outside the domain of the senses dealing with material things.[3]

There would of course be other voices that would more strongly condemn what they considered to be the unmitigated materialism of American life in this era, but on one point, there could be little argument: in the ingenuity of its mechanical inventions, America was unsurpassed. Patents registered in the United States during the year 1846 totaled just over 4,500; fifty years later, the number had increased to over 56,000 a year. Such figures prompted one commentator to conclude that fully nine-tenths of all the material riches and physical comforts enjoyed in 1896 had come into existence in the past fifty years.[4]

In the last third of the nineteenth century, the growth in the quantity of consumer products, together with much-improved means of distribution, created an unprecedented market for advertising in America. Much of this came in the form of increased newspaper and periodical advertising. Fundamentally, however, the way in which these media were used differed little from earlier in the century. Opportunities for illustration were extremely limited, and it was almost always in black and white. More significantly, many publishers of newspapers and magazines remained quite conservative in their dealings with advertisers, allowing only very restricted space to their advertising customers and excluding some kinds of products altogether. From the advertiser's standpoint, the two media which at the same time provided the greatest visual appeal and the most freedom from editorial constraints were the poster and the trade card. Both media proliferated rapidly in the 1880s, and both exploited the range of bright colors available in the chromolithographic process. Beyond this, these two forms of advertising had little in common. By its nature, the poster was a public medium, intended to be seen on walls of buildings or in store interiors. For many businesses, the use of posters lithographed in color was a relatively expensive proposition, and aside from those for circuses or theatrical events, most nineteenth-century examples were produced for products that sold in large volume on a national scale. Posters were particularly important for the promotion of beer and liquor since most magazines and newspapers of the period specifically excluded such advertising. The poster relied on bold imagery and brilliant colors for an immediate impression, with little in the way of explanatory text. By comparison, the trade card was essentially a private medium, either included in packages of the product or, more commonly, given away directly by local shopkeepers throughout the nation. No other medium could reach so many households, and no other one was saved and cherished by the consumers themselves. At the height of its popularity in the 1880s, the trade card was truly the most ubiquitous form of advertising in America. As one printing trade journal would remark in 1885, "the number of people who save handsome advertising cards when they chance to get them is larger now than ever and will increase with the growth of the population. No one is either so refined or so vulgar that he will not admire a pretty advertising card and save it. The ultimate destination of all cards is to swell some collection or to adorn some home, and they may be found in even the remotest parts of the land."[5]

There has been remarkably little scholarly literature on American advertising of the nineteenth century, and what does exist deals primarily with newspaper advertising or the poster. This study, which concentrates particularly on the heyday of the trade card in the 1880s and 1890s, will attempt to show how important this medium is as an indicator both of the consumer habits and of the social values of this dynamic era in America history. This survey can only begin to reveal the extraordinary range of products advertised by means of the trade card. Nevertheless, it will hopefully indicate that advertisers of the nineteenth century were far more resourceful and creative than they have previously been given credit for.

CHAPTER ONE

THE TRADE CARD IN THE SEVENTEENTH AND EIGHTEENTH CENTURIES

At the beginning of the seventeenth century, a city the size of London was the center of a number of highly competitive trades. Beyond the obvious desire to attract business away from one's competitors, merchants needed to inform customers of their location, and more specifically, to familiarize them with their personal shop sign. Since London streets were not numbered at this time, shop signs were the only means of locating a specific business address. Very few trade cards survive from the seventeenth century; the largest single collection was accumulated by Samuel Pepys before his death in 1703. Almost all of the forty-one cards in this group, which Pepys classified in his personal print collection under the heading of "Vulgaria," illustrate and name the shop sign of a London tradesman. The number of trades represented is quite varied, and aside from the intrinsic visual attraction of the signs and other imagery, the cards allow a partial reconstruction of the inner business district of London in the seventeenth century.[1]

In reference to examples from the seventeenth and eighteenth centuries, the use of the term *trade card* is somewhat misleading. These early specimens were not cards in the sense of being printed on heavy card or pasteboard; rather, they were usually printed on sheets of good quality paper, and ranged in size from a few inches up to folio dimensions. It is also important to consider that there was at first a rather nebulous distinction between trade cards proper and other printed business forms. The term *trade card* was never used in the seventeenth or eighteenth centuries, and those printers who supplied them usually referred to themselves as engravers of shopkeeper's bills.[2] Technically, bills and tradesmen's cards were different in format. When illustrated with a shopkeeper's sign or other device, bills usually left considerable space below for notations. They also generally contained phrases such as "bought of . . ." to indicate that the form was a receipt. Most eighteenth-century English bill forms carried insignia or other illustration only in the upper left corner.[3] In some cases, however, the same engraved plate was used for both trade cards and bill heads, the latter being printed on larger pieces of paper that had space for

writing below. To further complicate matters, tradesmen's cards themselves were often used as impromptu receipts or bills, as can be seen in the many cases where the back of the sheet is covered with writing indicating a transaction. In other instances, they might also have been used as labels and wrappers. Thus, while the printed forms loosely referred to as tradesmen's cards performed an important advertising function, providing information about the proprietor's location and line of wares, they could serve a number of other stationery uses as well.

In the seventeenth and eighteenth centuries, there were essentially two methods of printing trade cards. The more economical of the two was a combination of letterpress script and woodcut illustration. A striking example of this technique can be seen in a card for the London silk dyer John Edwards, printed around 1700 (Fig. 1). Here the Dove and Rainbow of the shopkeeper's sign serve as the unifying element in a simple but delightful landscape. Another rather bizarre card for a London coffinmaker, dating from around 1720, focuses on the tradesman's unusual

1. John Edwards, Silk Dyer, London. Anon. c. 1700. Woodcut and letterpress. 6 x 3¹/₄. The British Library.

2. Eleazar Malory, Joiner, London. Anon. c. 1720. Wood engraving. 5³/₄ x 3³/₄. The British Library.

of printing trade cards and other business forms in the eighteenth century was copperplate engraving. During much of the seventeenth century, England had lagged behind western Europe in engraving skills. When many Dutch engravers were brought in around the time of the Restoration, their presence undoubtedly helped to bring English engraving up to a very high standard. The number of skilled engravers working in London during the eighteenth century is reflected in the finely crafted cards they produced for an astonishingly wide variety of tradesmen. Some idea of this variety is provided in Ambrose Heal's classic study of tradesmen's cards of eighteenth-century London; among other curiosities, he cites cards for lunatic keepers, dog doctors, a prizefighter, a ratcatcher and sow gelder, a man-midwife (?), and purveyors of such goods as ass's milk, elephant teeth, and skeletons. One exterminator solemnly advertised himself as "Bugg Destroyer to his Majesty." A pork butcher offered "Sausages and Hogs Pudding of a Peculiar Flavour."[5]

While examples such as these provide an interesting and often humorous glimpse into the business life of eighteenth-century London, the main reason for the considerable attention that has been given to British trade cards of this period is the wealth of information they reveal about a group of luxury crafts and other highly specialized trades that themselves have been of great interest to historians and antiquarians. In terms of their quality and sheer numbers, the trade cards of furniture makers and goldsmiths are particularly important, and Heal has relied heavily on trade cards as a primary source of documentation in his

wares (Fig. 2). This card is also unusual in that both the illustrative material and the lettering below are printed from a single wood plate; no letterpress was used, even though the lettering is clearly in imitation of letterpress type.[4] By far the most common means

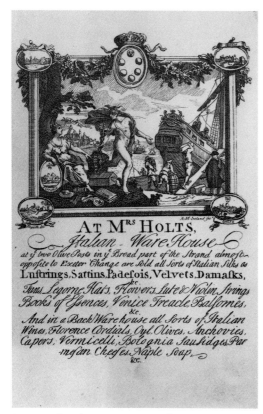

3. *Mrs. Holts Italian Ware House, London.* c. 1770. William Hogarth, designer, A. M. Ireland, engraver. 6³/₄ x 5. The British Museum.

4. *Richard Siddall, Chemist, London.* c. 1780. R. Clee, engraver. 10 x 7. The British Museum.

studies of these crafts.[6] In keeping with the elegance of the products they advertised, the design of furniture makers' and goldsmiths' cards of the later eighteenth century often featured *chinoiserie* and the elaborate rococo decoration associated with Thomas Chippendale and his highly influential *Gentleman and Cabinet-Maker's Director*, first published in 1754. Indeed, the overwhelming majority of cards illustrated in Heal's two studies of these trades exhibit this overall Chippendale influence.

Although trade cards of London booksellers and stationers were often quite elaborate, those of the engravers and printers themselves usually were not. This is somewhat surprising, since one would assume that in their own cards, engravers would want to show off the skills that they were advertising. William Hogarth's personal trade card was quite simple, even dull by later eighteenth-century standards, despite the fact that among the roughly thirty cards he designed for other businesses, some are very imaginative. Of particular interest is one for Mrs. Holt's "Italian Ware House" (Fig. 3), where the illustration takes the form of a flamboyantly baroque mythological scene in which Mercury takes his leave of a female personification of the city of Florence, as men load a ship in the background. The elegant frame is punctuated at its corners with landscape vignettes representing four other Italian cities. The lettering, executed in a wispy, cursive manner, extols the various exotic Italian imports offered by the proprietor. The design of the card was such that Hogarth and his printer could easily alter it to serve another patron by simply changing the text below. This he did on at least one occasion, when the same pictorial design was used in a bill head for a London wine merchant, dated 1772.[7] Even this paled by comparison to a large card by an engraver named R. Clee, one version of which carried an advertisement for a London druggist, dated 1781 (Fig. 4). Appropriately, it features a labyrinthine alchemist's lair worthy of the fantasies of Piranesi. As in the case of Hogarth's card, the written message is below, where it is inscribed in the folds of a great curtain. Here again, the same design was used in at least one other instance to advertise another business.[8]

With both the Hogarth and the Clee cards, there is still a reference to a shop sign; on the Clee card, the Golden Head of the establishment is represented at the top of the sheet. By the end of the eighteenth century, however, the depiction of shop signs on London trade cards had largely disappeared, and for an obvious reason: beginning in 1762, shop signs on the public streets were gradually removed by order of the city, and within ten years most of them had been replaced by numbered addresses. This is only the most obvious of the changes that had taken place in the design of British cards during the eighteenth century. In addition to becoming much more elaborate and sophisticated in their decorative detail, trade cards now carried much more descriptive information about the business concerned, reflecting a higher level of literacy among the urban public. Trade cards also became a much more widely used advertising medium, and the idea of designing plates on which inscriptions could be easily interchanged allowed printers to offer sophisticated designs to their patrons faster and more economically. By the end of the eighteenth century, the printing of trade cards had become a staple of the engraver's trade in London and a number of other British cities. Due to political vicissitudes as well as to differing business practices, trade cards were much less common on the European continent in the eighteenth century, although some examples printed in Paris have been mentioned in passing in studies of French paper ephemera.[9] The one other area in which the use of engraved trade

cards quickly caught on was in the American colonies. Given the economic links with the mother country and the fact that the first engravers and printers who worked in the colonies had been trained in England, it is not surprising that for most of the eighteenth century, trade cards printed in America closely followed the patterns established in London.

Aside from a few crude woodcuts, printmaking scarcely existed in the American colonies until the early eighteenth century. Francis Dewing is considered to have brought the first professional copperplate printing press to the colonies from England in 1717. As late as 1750, there may have been as few as five such presses in America.[10] However, it was not long from the time this printing technology was introduced that it was used for the printing of trade cards and other business forms. The earliest known example, dating from about 1727, was probably printed by Thomas Johnson, a craftsman of various trades who was born in Boston around 1708. The card advertised the bookstore of Thomas Hancock, uncle of John Hancock, and pictures Hancock's shop sign, the Bible and Three Crowns.[11] The Boston engraver and silversmith James Turner went a step further when, in a card for the hardware merchants Joseph and Daniel Waldo, he featured their sign of the Elephant with an elaborate wrought-iron bracket. The pole from which this is hung takes up the entire left margin of the print (Fig. 5). Especially interesting in this card is the astonishingly large inventory of goods, most of which were imported from England, that were advertised for sale. This list would seem to indicate that even in the most impor-

5. *Joseph and Daniel Waldo, Merchants, Boston.* c. 1748. James Turner, engraver. 9¼ x 6⅛. American Antiquarian Society.

tant trading city of the American colonies, business was not nearly so specialized as in London. The card stresses the wholesale side of the Waldo business, mentioning as a last note that "Country Traders & Shopkeepers may be as well serv'd by Letters as if

6. *Philip Godfrid Kast, Druggist, Salem.* c. 1774.
Nathaniel Hurd, engraver. 7¼ x 5½. American
Antiquarian Society.

present Themselves." The Waldo brothers were not
associated in business until 1748, and since an issue of
the *Boston Gazette* listed an almost identical line of
their goods in 1749,[12] it is likely that the card was
printed in one of these two years, perhaps in an effort
to introduce the new business to the Boston public.

Turner himself apparently left Boston for Philadelphia shortly thereafter.

Little is known of the trade card engravers working in New England prior to 1750, and those that can
be identified are known by only a handful of examples. In the case of Nathaniel Hurd, however, we
encounter an individual who produced and signed a
considerable amount of commercial work. Born in
Boston in 1729, he was also a silversmith. Hurd is
known particularly for his bookplates, the earliest of
which dates from around 1749. He signed at least
thirty different bookplates, and a number of others
are attributed to him.[13] In keeping with this category
of engraving, many of the plates are quite formal and
heraldic in nature, but there are also enough examples
that feature fanciful Chippendale-style borders to
indicate that Hurd was quite familiar with current
trends in English fashion and printing. Given this
degree of sophistication, it is somewhat surprising
that, as indicated by a handwritten notation at the
bottom of one print, the trade card he printed for the
Salem druggist Philip Godfrid Kast (Fig. 6) should
date from as late as 1774. Although less cluttered in
its design, this card obviously has the same general
format as the earlier one by Turner, even down to the
note at the bottom appealing to the country trade.
This card is significant, however, as a very early
advertisement for what would later be known as
patent medicines. The mention of Turlington's Balsam of Life, Hooper's Female Pills, and various other
remedies suggests that several concoctions imported
from Britain were already known and purchased by
name in the colonies.

Among the silversmiths and other craftsmen
engaged in copperplate engraving in eighteenth-century Boston, none is better known than Paul Revere.
Revere kept extensive records of his daily business
transactions, and interspersed in these daybooks are
numerous references to orders for various printed
business cards and forms, none of which have survived. Thus it appears that those few trade cards by
Revere that have been found represent only a fraction
of his total output.[14] The limited evidence indicates
that among the prerevolutionary engravers working
in Boston, Revere was especially fond of elaborate
Chippendale motifs. This influence is not difficult to
explain since at least twenty-nine copies of Chippendale's *Gentleman and Cabinet-Maker's Director* are
believed to have been in the colonies prior to the Revolution, along with several other manuals patterned
after it.[15] In at least one case, Revere directly copied a
British trade card. The overall design and decorative
detail of the card he engraved for the Boston importer
William Breck (Fig. 7) are identical to that found on
an unsigned card for Joseph Welch, a hardware merchant of London. This card also seems to have served
as the model for another card attributed to Revere.[16]
From the evidence of his daybooks, Revere did several
printing jobs for Breck, although this particular card
is not listed among them. The Breck trade card could
not have been printed later than 1770 since Breck
signed a handwritten bill dated that year on the back
of the specimen held by the American Antiquarian
Society.

Although the earliest American trade cards may
have been printed in Boston, in the later eighteenth

century Philadelphia seems to have produced the most elaborate ones. This degree of sophistication is partly due to the fact that several of the most noted copperplate engravers working in Philadelphia had immigrated directly from England. Henry Dawkins arrived in America around 1753 and, after spending a few years in New York, settled in Philadelphia in 1757. Like Hurd, Dawkins did a number of book plates, but those by Dawkins show little imagination. They are almost invariably laden with heavy Chippendale-style ornament and were probably derived from British book plates Dawkins had seen.[17] As in the case of Revere, Dawkins on at least one occasion modeled a trade card after an English example. The overall design of the card for the Philadelphia coppersmith Benjamin Harbeson (Fig. 8) is the same as one made by an English engraver named Warner for the London razormaker Henry Patten. Only the objects suspended from the terminal ornaments and the lettering have been changed.[18] Dawkins's propensity for copying the work of others eventually got him into considerable trouble; he was arrested in New York in 1776 on charges of counterfeiting, which at the time was a capital offense. In a long appeal written from prison during that year, Dawkins complained that he preferred a hasty execution over the wretched conditions in which he was being kept.[19] Fortunately, he was subsequently released, and there is even a record of his having been paid by the Continental Congress for some bill engraving work he did in 1780.

One of the most gifted copperplate engravers active in Philadelphia was John Smither, who first

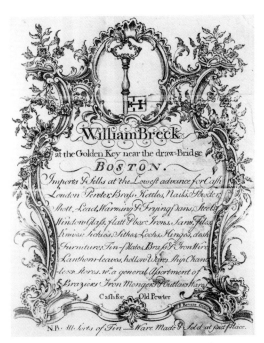

7. *William Breck, Merchant, Boston.* c. 1770. Paul Revere, engraver. 7 x 5⅜ to edge of plate mark. American Antiquarian Society.

8. *Benjamin Harbeson, Coppersmith, Philadelphia.* c. 1775. Henry Dawkins, engraver. 7⁵/₁₆ x 6³/₁₆ to edge of plate mark. Henry Francis du Pont Winterthur Museum.

worked there from around 1768 to 1778. Smither immigrated from London, where he had already developed considerable skills as an engraver and gunsmith. A remarkable example of Smither's engraving talents is the trade card he produced for Benjamin Randolph, a Philadelphia cabinetmaker (Fig. 9). This card, surely one of the most flamboyant of any printed in eighteenth-century America,

includes a Chippendale-style framework, but does not seem to have been modeled after any British trade card. The card provides an excellent record of the aristocratic taste in American furniture of the late colonial period, as well as an indication of the specific design sources that influenced that taste. In a careful examination of the Randolph trade card, Fiske Kimball has determined that while some pieces of furniture resemble designs in Chippendale's *Director,* more of them can be traced to another English design manual, *Household Furniture in the Present Taste,* which was available in America by 1760. The tall clock pictured in the upper right corner of the card came from yet another source, Thomas Johnson's *Designs for Furniture* of 1758. Thus there are three specific sources for the variety of elegant furniture illustrated on Randolph's trade card.[20] To further accentuate the aristocratic appeal of the card, Smither introduced intricate architectural embellishments in the upper portion of the print, including both neoclassical and Gothic elements.

Smither's versatility in supplying the needs of his business clients can be seen in the great contrast between the flamboyance of the Randolph card and another well-known example that he engraved about the same time. By comparison to practically any other example from the colonial period, the card Smither printed for Francis Hopkinson (Fig. 10) is the essence of straightforward simplicity. The small pastoral landscape vignette with sheep is not enclosed within any ornamental borders, and the nicely varied lettering of the message below is arranged in a few well-balanced lines. This trade card must have been done very soon after Smither's arrival in Philadelphia, since on its back Hopkinson wrote out a bill for cloth goods dated September 1769.[21] Hopkinson's card has attracted attention not only for its intrinsic charm, but also because of the historical significance of the patron. Hopkinson would become far more than a

9. *Benjamin Randolph, Cabinet Maker, Philadelphia.* c. 1770. John Smither, engraver. 9¹/₈ x 7¹/₈. Library Company of Philadelphia.

10. *Francis Hopkinson, Merchant, Philadelphia.* c. 1768. John Smither, engraver. 8³/₄ x 7. The New-York Historical Society.

modest cloth merchant. Trained in law, he was a member of the Continental Congress and was on the committee that drafted the Declaration of Independence. His signature on that document is identical to the one on the trade card, which had been printed several years earlier. Smither himself clearly differed in his political sympathies. Having allegedly counterfeited Pennsylvania currency for the British, he was

accused of treason and hurriedly left Philadelphia in the company of British troops in 1777, settling in New York. Several years after the Revolutionary War, he returned to Philadelphia, where he lived out his remaining years.

Even after the Revolution, many trade cards printed in America continued to show the frilly rococo decoration seen in those by Revere, Dawkins, and others. In a few cases, however, attention to land-scape elements served to mitigate such affectations, and perhaps also hint of at least a slight departure from British influences. In this regard, a design engraved by David Tew for Edward Pole (Fig. 11), a fishing tackle maker of Philadelphia, makes an interesting transitional piece. Very little is known about Tew's career; he was established in business in Philadelphia by 1780, and eight years later was mentioned in the journals of the Continental Congress as being owed a sum of money for some bank notes he had engraved. The card engraved for Edward Pole probably dates from the 1780s, and is no later than 1788, since the specimen owned by the Historical Society of Pennsylvania has a bill on the back written in that year. On this card the ostentatious Chippendale border motifs are still present, but it is to the rectangular landscape scene on the upper portion of the card that the eye is immediately drawn. In the foreground, a presumed customer of Mr. Pole is reeling in a fish, while his companion waits at the edge of the pond with a net. It has been pointed out that the fish dangling rather curiously on the terminal ornaments of the border decoration closely resemble one in the woodcut illustration of an advertisement placed by Pole in a local newspaper in 1784. Anonymous woodcut illustrations appeared in American newspapers throughout the eighteenth century, but in this case, it would appear that there is a specific connection with a trade card engraver. The wood block for the newspaper advertisement could have been cut by Tew himself, or it might have been modeled after one of his trade cards by someone else.[22]

11. *Edward Pole, Fishing Tackle Maker, Philadelphia.* c. 1785. David Tew, engraver. 9 x 6⅞. Historical Society of Pennsylvania.

12. *Ebenezer Larkin, Bookseller and Stationer, Boston.* c. 1790. Engraving. 9 x 6½. The New-York Historical Society.

By the end of the eighteenth century, American engravers were increasingly breaking away from the decorative intricacies and other conventions they had inherited from the tradition of British trade cards. Their growing independence in approaches to pictorial content can be seen especially in their emphasis on the physical environment around them. The idea of depicting the actual place of business of the adver-tiser was not completely original to American trade cards; one can occasionally encounter eighteenth-century British examples as well. However, trade cards featuring stores, shops, and other architectural subjects became especially common in America. The most straightforward approach, and one that would be especially common in the early nineteenth century, was to represent the street facade of the business being advertised, sometimes including a selection of the merchant's wares in the windows. A fascinating trade card printed for Ebenezer Larkin's Boston book and stationery business went a step further, actually bringing the viewer directly into the interior of the shop (Fig. 12). Surrounded by shelves crammed with books and supplies, a clerk waits on two elegantly dressed customers. There is no indication as to who engraved or printed this card, but it probably dates from around 1790 since shortly thereafter Larkin moved his business to a different location down the street. Larkin apparently shared the address indicated on this card with Paul Revere.[23] According to his records, Revere was still engraving various business forms in the 1790s, but it is unlikely that he did this card. He would probably have signed it, and neither the fastidious detail nor the lettering style resembles anything Revere is known to have produced.

One of the most extraordinary trade cards depicting an architectural subject that survives from around the turn of the century is the one for Prince Stetson's Tavern in Newburyport, Massachusetts (Fig. 13). As indicated directly below the image, William Hooker was both designer and engraver of this card. Hooker had worked in Philadelphia until 1804, where he had specialized in the engraving of maps and charts. He

was in Newburyport between 1805 and 1810, and the Stetson card was presumably printed some time during these years. Although Hooker is hardly a well-known engraver, this trade card shows unusually strong composition and attention to detail for this period. A portrait of James Wolfe, the British general killed at Montreal during the French and Indian Wars, is clearly visible on the hanging sign in front of the inn. On the street, a carriage drawn by four horses enters from the left. To the right, a gentleman accompanies an elegantly attired lady riding sidesaddle. Yet what is perhaps most remarkable is Hooker's sensitivity to light, and how it is expressed in the engraving. The tavern itself is scarcely distinguished as architecture, but the contrast between the side in bright daylight and the one in shadow gives a crisp definition to the whole. Even the horses in the foreground cast individual shadows. Perhaps more than any other example, Hooker's trade card for the Prince Stetson Tavern shows how much progress had been made in this field of printing in the less than one hundred years it had been practiced in America. In the early years of the nineteenth century, American trade cards might become more technically sophisticated and be printed by more skillful engravers, but few would exhibit the honest observation and animation shown here.

13. *Prince Stetson and Company Tavern, Newburyport*. c. 1805. William Hooker, engraver. 8¼ x 5¼. American Antiquarian Society.

THE EVOLUTION
OF THE AMERICAN TRADE CARD
IN THE NINETEENTH CENTURY

At the beginning of the nineteenth century, the production and use of trade cards in America generally followed the same patterns established in the eighteenth century. Most cards were still made by copperplate engravers working in the urban centers of Boston, New York, and Philadelphia. However, as native industries and communication between different regions continued to develop, trade cards began to be used by a wider variety of merchants and manufacturers and appeared over a larger geographical area. The style and imagery employed in the cards also evolved rapidly in this period. As with British work, American engravers abandoned flamboyant rococo decoration in favor of the more solemn and restrained motifs of neoclassicism, with a particular emphasis on architectural elements and the human figure. This coincided with the increasing use of patriotic symbols, a trend undoubtedly reinforced by the unifying influence of the War of 1812.

An especially prolific trade card printer at the beginning of the nineteenth century was Abel Bowen. Bowen was a copperplate engraver and book publisher who began working in Boston around

1805. By 1812, he had established his own printing business. Bowen's personal engraving style may not have been especially subtle, but it was characterized by a firm, bold line and strong contours. A card Bowen printed for a Boston furrier and hatter (Fig. 14) uses another variation on the allegorical female figure, who has not only the pole and hat but also the shield of the union, a standard attribute of Columbia. The eagle flies above a banner inscribed "under this we shall prosper." Particularly notable is the presence of the American Indian holding the pelt on the left side, as if to indicate a noble savage counterpart to the craftsman holding the hat on the right. The foliage surrounding the three figures suggests the unspoiled, primeval forest from which the Indian has emerged. Bowen used the same elements, minus the hatmaker, in a card for another Boston hatter. In several other trade cards, including his own, Bowen emphasized landscape backgrounds.[1] As seen in his card for the furrier John Bordman, he also reduced the inscription to the barest essentials, usually placing it in an open area such as an architectural pedestal.

A card with an even more emblematic and classical

14. *John Bordman, Hatter and Furrier, Boston.* c. 1815. Abel Bowen, engraver. 4³/₈ x 3³/₄. American Antiquarian Society.

15. *Phineas Cole, Manufacturer, Brattleborough.*
c. 1830. John Chorley, engraver. 5⁷/₈ x 7¹/₄. The
New-York Historical Society.

16. *J. Brewster, Hat Maker, New York.* c. 1820.
Peter Maverick, engraver. 4⁵/₁₆ x 2¹/₂ to edge of
plate mark. The New-York Historical Society.

flavor was engraved by John Chorley for Phineas Cole, a manufacturer of "Brattleborough," Vermont (Fig. 15). Chorley began working in Boston around 1825 but was only listed as an engraver in the city directories between 1831 and 1834. This trade card shows the increasing tendency for engravers in the major urban centers to produce cards for businessmen and manufacturers in outlying but rapidly industrializing regions. The design of this finely detailed card had the obvious advantage of allowing the engraver to inscribe the name and address of different customers by a simple reworking of the area within the pedestal on the copper plate. Engravers almost always retained the copper plates from which their jobs had been printed, and these were undoubtedly reused in a number of ways. This practice anticipates

the stock trade cards, printed in such profusion later in the century, which were purchased in bulk by any number of retailers. The small scale and format of this card are similar to those of a bookplate, and while

patriotic imagery may not have been as evident in bookplates of this period, one can observe the same general evolution from the frilly rococo of the eighteenth century to the neoclassical simplicity of the postrevolutionary period.[2] Just as it had been with Hurd and Revere, the bookplate remained a staple product of copperplate engravers in the early nineteenth century.

By the early years of the nineteenth century, more American copperplate printers were specializing in commercial work than ever before. Nowhere was this more evident than in New York, where in the engraving of trade cards the Maverick family holds a position of special importance. Peter Maverick was perhaps the single most prolific engraver of trade cards in New York during the first years of the century. Peter trained with his father, Peter Rushton Maverick, and they collaborated in the printing of a number of bookplates. This may help explain why Peter Maverick, like Chorley, often produced trade cards of an emblematic nature. On a card for a New York hatmaker (Fig. 16) Maverick placed the figures of Columbia and the American eagle on a huge pedestal. Another Maverick card, exactly the same except for the message inscribed within the pedestal, was printed for another hatmaker in Norfolk, Virginia.[3] This card is signed "P. Maverick & Durand N. York," and thus must have been printed during Peter Maverick's brief partnership with his former apprentice, Asher B. Durand, between 1818 and 1820. This example demonstrates that Maverick, who by this time had built a substantial commercial engraving business in the New York area, was also able to mar-

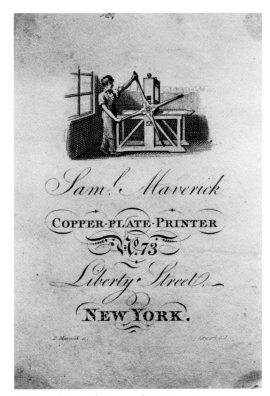

17. *Samuel Maverick, Copper-Plate Printer, New York.* c. 1815. Peter Maverick, engraver. 3⁵/₁₆ x 2³/₄. The New-York Historical Society.

ket his trade cards to merchants over a wide geographical area. Peter Maverick is important not only for the variety of cards he printed for other tradesmen, but also for the ones he made to advertise his own business and that of his brothers. A card for his

half-brother Samuel (Fig. 17) shows a printer at work on a large star-wheel press such as Samuel or Peter might have used in this period. Peter, who had a reputation as a master of "writing engraving," certainly shows those skills on Samuel's trade card. Samuel went on to engrave a number of trade cards himself, although he was not nearly so prolific as Peter.

Another prolific trade card printer working in New York just after the turn of the century was John Scoles, an engraver best known for his views of New York City buildings and his landscape prints. In Scoles's designs we find a delicate, flowing quality largely lacking in other American trade cards of the period. A card he did for a New York painter named

18. *Thomas McGary, Painter and Glazier, New York.* c. 1815. John Scoles, engraver. 3¹/₈ x 4⁵/₈. The New-York Historical Society.

Thomas McGary is fascinating in that it actually pictures the artist at work (Fig. 18). That McGary is shown working in an inviting coastal landscape apparently has nothing to do with what he is painting. The image vaguely visible on his easel is a large eagle, probably destined to become a hanging sign for a New York merchant. On his card for the Brott and Snow dry goods store (Fig. 19), Scoles again included a trading ship in the background, but here the emphasis is on the two graceful, classically garbed women holding a garland over the inscription. The figure holding the scales on the right is almost identical in pose to the single figure used in Scoles's own trade card, which is full of classical references. Inter-

19. *Brott and Snow, Dry Goods, New York.* c. 1815. John Scoles, engraver. 3⅛ x 4⅝. The New-York Historical Society.

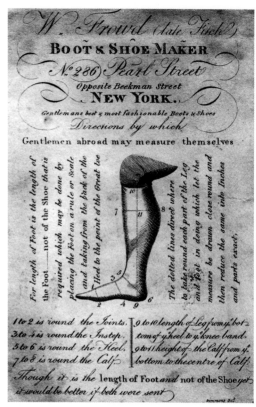

20. *W. Frowd, Boot and Shoe Maker, New York.* c. 1815. Simmons (Abraham?), engraver. 4⅝ x 3⅛. The New-York Historical Society.

estingly, the two female figures on the Brott and Snow card are arranged in exactly the same manner as the Liberty and Justice figures William Rollinson used for a merchant's trade card from around 1800.[4] Scoles and Rollinson probably drew from a common source—most likely British—for this composition. Just as with American imitations of British ornamental affectations in the eighteenth century, there are close parallels between the neoclassical trappings of early nineteenth-century American cards and those produced in England.

The general tendency in early nineteenth-century trade cards was toward monumental and uncluttered compositions that included little in the way of a writ-ten message beyond the name and address of the advertiser. There are exceptions, however, as can be seen in a rather curious card printed for a New York bootmaker (Fig. 20). Here the engraver went to enormous labor to engrave the copious instructions by which "Gentlemen Abroad" could measure themselves. The name *Simmons* at the bottom of the card indicates the engraver. This may have been the work of Abraham Simmons, an engraver about whom virtually nothing is known except that he worked in New York briefly in 1814–1815. In any case, the message of the card clearly suggests that it was distributed widely, and indeed played a key role in this early mail-order business.

Philadelphia remained a leading center for copperplate printing in the early nineteenth century, producing some of the most original and imaginative

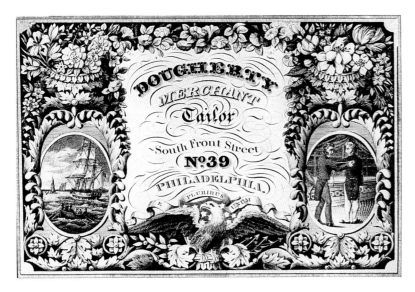

21. *Alexander Dougherty, Tailor, Philadelphia.* c. 1830. Tiller (Robert?), engraver. 3 x 4½. The New-York Historical Society.

either inventiveness or execution.

There are other trade card printers of the early nineteenth century who are fascinating precisely for their parochial and naive qualities. The case of William Hamlin is interesting not only because a good deal is known about him, but also because he produced several trade cards for his own business. Born in 1772, Hamlin worked in relative isolation in Providence, Rhode Island, where he died in 1869 at the age of ninety-seven. A jack-of-all-trades, Hamlin was apparently self-taught in engraving and probably made most of his own tools. The dating of the several cards advertising his business is extremely difficult, especially since his designs do not follow the major stylistic trends evident in urban centers. One possible clue is the fact that in 1809 Hamlin's son joined him in establishing an instrument-making business. One trade card engraved by Hamlin and owned by the American Antiquarian Society advertises the variety of goods offered by W. and J. H. Hamlin, including jewelry, fancy goods, and musical instruments, as well as the services of engraving and printing.[5] It is therefore possible, although by no means certain, that the cards on which William Hamlin indicated himself as the sole proprietor were engraved before 1809. Like so many naive painters of nineteenth-century America, Hamlin was primarily concerned with conveying the visual facts of his immediate environment. One of Hamlin's cards includes his place of business in Providence, with his shop sign, the quadrant, shown on the side of the building (Fig. 22). Interestingly, in this example, Hamlin advertised himself only as a manufacturer and repairer of instru-

trade cards of the period. Here there seems to have been a particular emphasis on landscape elements for their own sake. In contrast to the more formal and classical style of Peter Maverick and others, there was also a general tendency to fill up the card with a wealth of ornamental detail. This latter characteristic is strikingly evident in the trade card of the Philadelphia tailor Alexander Dougherty (Fig. 21). On the basis of Dougherty's street address in the city directory, this card can be from no earlier than 1823. The engraver's name, Tiller, is inscribed on the card. However, there were in fact three Tillers active as engravers in Philadelphia in the early nineteenth century. Robert Tiller, an engraver of landscape views, is

only listed in the city directory from 1818 to 1824; it is more likely that the card was made either by his son, also named Robert, or by Frederick Tiller, who was active from 1831 until 1850. Whoever the designer may have been, on this card he masterfully combined the common images of the ship and the eagle with a scene in a tailor's shop and masses of floral ornamentation used to create a spectacular enframement for the elegantly lettered inscription. The sheer profusion of detail belies the relatively small dimensions of the card, only four-and-a-half by three inches. It is certainly one of the most elaborate trade cards to be engraved in America to this point, indicating that Philadelphia engravers were not to be outdone in

22. *William Hamlin, Nautical and Optical Instruments, Providence.* c. 1810. William Hamlin, engraver. 3¼ x 4⅜. The New-York Historical Society.

ments, not as an engraver. By the standards of the engravers working in New York or Philadelphia, Hamlin's trade cards seem extremely crude. Yet there is an animation in this depiction of the dockside activity of Providence that seems in retrospect to compensate for Hamlin's lack of technical sophistication.

In the overall history of trade cards, work by Hamlin and copperplate engravers of similarly modest talents represents a vanishing breed. For a hundred years, American craftsmen who had usually specialized in metal smithing, instrument-making, or other technical skills had turned out trade cards for themselves and other businessmen primarily as a sideline. Even for Peter Maverick, who was a specialist in

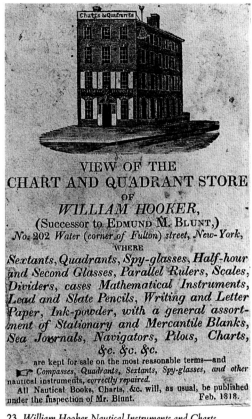

23. *William Hooker, Nautical Instruments and Charts, New York.* 1818. Wood engraving. 6 x 3¾. The New-York Historical Society.

copperplate engraving, trade cards represent a relatively small percentage of his total output. Personalized trade cards by local engravers were

undoubtedly justifiable enough as an advertising expense for many merchants of the eighteenth and early nineteenth centuries. In most cases, however, these cards must have been distributed in relatively small numbers. It must be remembered that in the case of cards made from engraved copper plates, each specimen had to be pulled one at a time on a hand-operated press, and between each printing, the copper plate needed to be carefully inked and wiped by a trained worker. At the beginning of the nineteenth century, there was no alternative to this painstaking process except the letterpress, on which metal type and a wood block for the illustration could be combined. The wood engraving remained the sole means of illustrating advertisements in newspapers. The process of stereotyping—the casting of engraved wood blocks in metal—allowed for the mass syndication of certain standard woodcuts for use in newspapers everywhere. While the letterpress could make trade cards more quickly and more cheaply than was possible with copperplate printing, the cards themselves were not nearly so fine in detail. Even though the lettering was a much simpler matter, whenever a wood block illustration had to be prepared for a specific customer, there was still a good deal of labor involved. As distinct from unillustrated calling cards, which were also generally printed by letterpress, the trade cards illustrated with wood engraving were more common in smaller towns, where the skills of the copperplate engraver were not readily accessible. Still, the quality of craftsmanship evident in some of these cards is impressive. A good example is the card by an unknown printer for the chart and instrument

24. *Elihu Geer, Steam Job and Card Printer, Hartford.* 1860. E Bolles, engraver. Wood engraving with metal type. 3 x 2¹/₄. The Warshaw Collection of Business Americana, Smithsonian Institution.

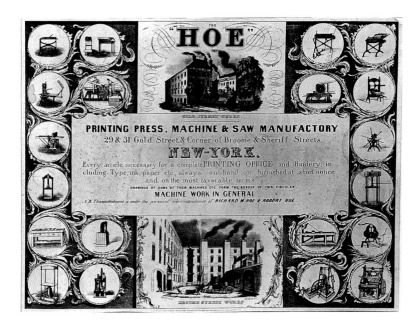

25. *Hoe Company Printing Press, Machine and Saw Manufactury, New York.* Advertisement Circular. 1847. Endicott, Lithographer. 19 x 25. Museum of the City of New York.

business of William Hooker of New York, dated 1818 (Fig. 23). Like many eighteenth-century cards, this gives an extensive account of Hooker's offerings, along with a reasonably detailed illustration of his business building. Cards combining metal type and wood-engraved illustrations continued to be quite common in provincial areas as late as the Civil War. A card for Elihu Geer, printer and stationer of Hartford, Connecticut, has a calendar for the year on the reverse side, and can thus be specifically dated to 1860 (Fig. 24). While the use of both sides of the card became the rule with chromolithographed trade cards of the later nineteenth century, this is an early example of the practice on a wood-engraved card. It is also interesting to note the variety of goods and services listed on this card. Among other things, Geer advertised himself as a "steam job and card printer." By this point, steam power had long since become established in standard letterpresses, although for printers working on a small scale it was not necessarily practical. For more modest operations, American manufacturers offered a wide variety of manual presses by midcentury, eliminating the need for the more expensive imported presses that had dominated the trade in the late eighteenth and early nineteenth centuries. An indication of the variety of printing equipment available from American manufacturers around midcentury can be seen in a circular distributed in 1847 by the Hoe Manufacturing Company, the largest domestic supplier of presses for the trade (Fig. 25). In the years just before the Civil War, most business stationery printed in small towns was done on smaller, manual presses such as these by local printers who were responsible for all the printing needs of the community.

Although both engraving and letterpress methods would be employed to some extent in manufacturing trade cards after midcentury, the real future of the trade card was with an entirely new printing technology introduced in America in the early years of the century. The lithographic process was invented by Alois Senefelder in Bavaria in 1798. This process resulted from Senefelder's experiments in using a particularly smooth variety of local Bavarian limestone to replace copper plates in commercial printing. However, Senefelder soon discovered that if he first drew on the surface of the stone with a greasy crayon, then poured a thin gum arabic solution over the entire surface, and finally covered it with ink, only the greased area took the ink. This printing method, based on the simple principle that grease and water do not mix, was truly planographic—relying on a chemical action of the surface, rather than making marks or grooves in a plate as with engraving and etching. Once the lithographic stone had been drawn upon, gummed, and inked, the remainder of the process was not that different from copperplate printing, except that special care had to be taken in applying pressure over the moistened paper to avoid breaking the stone. Senefelder discovered that he could make as many prints as he wished from a properly prepared lithographic stone. The size of the print depended primarily on the capability of the press to accommodate the weight of the stone. From the artist's standpoint, it was far easier and faster to draw on the

surface of the stone than to engrave a metal surface.

Within ten years of Senefelder's invention of lithography, the special Solenhofen limestone slabs that were critical to the process were being imported into America. Try as they might, American printers were unable to find any stone that could be ground to a surface smooth enough to be a viable substitute. Indeed, in the early years of the century, American lithographers were not only reliant on imported lithographic stones, but on foreign lithograph presses and inks as well.[6] Nevertheless, lithography as a commercial printing process spread rapidly in America. The first major lithographic firm was that of William S. and John B. Pendleton of Boston. In 1825 William was working as an engraver in partnership with Abel Bowen. That same year, his younger brother John returned from a stay in Paris, where he had studied lithographic techniques. The brothers immediately established a lithographic printing business in Boston, and in addition to printing, sold a variety of lithographic equipment to others trying to break into this new business.[7] They also hired and trained two men who would be extremely important in the future history of American lithography: Nathaniel Currier and John H. Bufford. John Pendleton did not stay in Boston very long, traveling first to Philadelphia, where he worked with Kearney and Childs in 1828–1829, and then to New York, where he had a lithographic business from 1829 to 1834. He then sold out to his former pupil Currier. While extremely important in disseminating lithographic technology in Boston and other cities, the Pendletons do not seem to have used the process to print many trade

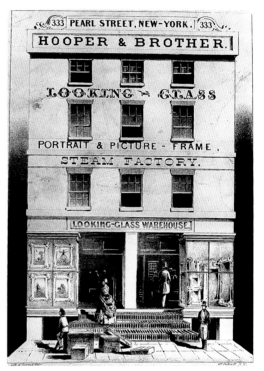

26. *Hooper and Brother Looking Glass Warehouse, New York.* c. 1849. Sarony and Major, lithographers. 12 x 9½. Museum of the City of New York.

cards, although there is one attractive card showing a warehouse for a glass company in Charleston, South Carolina, in the New-York Historical Society Collection.[8] After his brother's departure, William stayed in the lithographic business only until 1836. After

27. *F. Basham, Modeller, Plaster, Cement and Scagliola Worker, New York.* 1844. E. Jones, lithographer. 21 x 13⅜. Museum of the City of New York.

selling this business, he subsequently worked primarily in the field of bank-note engraving.

One advantage of lithography over an intaglio process such as copperplate engraving was that large prints that still had considerable detail could be produced quickly and in large numbers. This advantage coincided with an awakening early nineteenth-century interest in the topographical documentation of America. Within a few years of the introduction of lithography in this country, it was employed to turn out an enormous variety of city views and picturesque landscapes. This was especially true in New York, which soon outdistanced any other city in the number of practitioners in the lithographic trade. New York City had as many as sixty lithography firms by 1854,[9] and while some came and went over the years, others lasted for several decades. A firm particularly important for its documentation of New York City businesses in this period was Sarony, Major and Knapp. In its heyday just before the Civil War, this company was unquestionably the top firm in this highly competitive industry in New York. It began in 1846, when Napoleon Sarony joined with the Major family to form the original company, which went by the names of Sarony and Company or Sarony and Major until Joseph Knapp joined the firm in 1857. The name was changed to Major and Knapp after the withdrawal of Sarony from the business in 1864.

From early in their collaboration, Sarony and Major printed a variety of advertisement sheets for New York City businesses. Sometimes referred to as trade cards, these lithographic prints are in fact closer to the size of broadsides, often measuring twelve by fifteen inches or larger. These prints typically consist of a straightforward view of the facade of the retail establishment. As we see in an example Sarony and Major printed for a local mirror and framing company (Fig. 26), these cards often illustrate various goods in the shop windows and the comings and goings of pedestrians on the street. Like smaller trade cards, these lithographs were given out by merchants and were useful in introducing prospective customers to a new business or to one that had just changed locations. Sometimes such lithographs also appeared in city directories, as with the many views that Sarony, Major and Knapp did for the *Manual of the City Common Council of New York.*[10] In Philadelphia, which had been the first American city to publish a city directory, large lithographs of store fronts and factories were even more common, yielding a unique architectural record of this rapidly expanding industrial center in the years before the Civil War.[11] Although probably less accurate as an architectural record, certain cards, particularly those that advertised businesses in the larger cities, sometimes provide interesting views of business interiors of the period. One highly unusual example printed by an E. Jones in 1844 shows the cluttered showroom of a New York maker of decorative sculpture (Fig. 27). Even more curious is the card advertising Dr. Gutmann's Russian Vapor Baths (Fig. 28). There is nothing in this little scene to suggest what is specifically Russian about these baths, but whatever their qualities, men had the monopoly on them most of the time; the facilities were open to ladies only between the hours of 10:00 and 12:00 a.m. The provincial businesses that were rapidly developing in this period were particularly dependent on the physical appeal of the architectural premises, and it is probable that a great many of the hotels and roadhouses that sprouted up in outlying areas were widely advertised by means of the illustrated trade card. The

28. *Dr. Gutmann's Russian Vapor Baths, New York.* c. 1850. Lithograph. 5¼ x 6½. The New-York Historical Society.

the great lengths gone to by some lithographers to advertise their services. Based on the fact that all three partners are listed, an elegant and extraordinarily detailed card by Sarony, Major and Knapp (Fig. 30) can be dated to the years between 1857 and 1864. The four vignettes with female figures, along with the elaborate ornamental detail and lettering, indicate that the firm wished to stress the artistic side of their lithography business. Barely visible below the central area of lettering is a tiny oval containing what appears to be the interior of their establishment at 449 Broadway. The message, however, stresses the firm's services as "practical lithographers," including not only the city views for which the company is well known, but also show cards, maps, plans, and "labels of every description." The trade card of general lithographer Jacob Seibert (Fig. 31) is much less elaborate, but goes into greater detail describing his offerings in the area of commercial printing. The "show cards" mentioned on both of these cards refer to larger lithographic prints that would have been used primarily for posting or window display. Interestingly, at the bottom of the Seibert trade card there is an additional handwritten message: "all kinds of engraving done for the trade." In this period, most of the major lithographic firms continued to offer printing from metal plates as a sideline.

Lithographers in Philadelphia around midcentury may not have been as numerous as in New York, but they were no less competitive and no less anxious to show off their skills in their personal trade cards. More than anywhere else, lithography in Philadelphia was established by foreign-born artists.

anonymous but finely crafted card for the Messenger House of Cortland (Fig. 29) gives us a glimpse of an architectural highlight of this burgeoning town in central New York State around 1860. Quite aside from the attractions of such a sophisticated piece of printing, this kind of architectural record makes it all the more unfortunate that so few trade cards for businesses like the Messenger House have survived.

Before leaving the subject of trade cards in the pre–Civil War period, a few words should be added about the category of cards which, with the introduction of lithographic technology, showed the greatest change from the days of copperplate printing: the trade cards of the commercial printers themselves. The versatility of the medium itself created many new possibilities for lithographers, especially in the area of original landscape prints and art reproductions. It also allowed them to produce a more varied and attractive range of business-related printing than most engravers could offer. Such versatility, together with the competitive pressures created by the sheer abundance of lithographers after 1830, accounts for

MESSENGER HOUSE.
Cortland, N.Y.
W.ᵐ S. COPELAND, PROPRIETOR.
Applications received at this House for the use of the new MESSENGER HALL.

29. *Messenger House, Cortland, New York.* c. 1860. Lithograph. 2³/₄ x 4¹/₄. Author's collection.

30. *Sarony, Major and Knapp Lithographers, New York.* c. 1860. Sarony, Major and Knapp, lithographers. 8³/₄ x 5¹/₄. The Warshaw Collection of Business Americana, Smithsonian Institution.

Augustus Koellner (sometimes spelled *Kollner*) was born in Dusseldorf, Germany, and emigrated to the United States around 1839; he would be active in Philadelphia until the 1870s. Koellner was especially interested in landscape, and it could be argued that his European romanticism and sense of wonder at the American landscape inspired his interpretation of that subject in a manner not seen in most native-born landscapists. He was not only a lithographer, but also a skilled engraver and landscape painter in watercolor, traveling widely in frontier areas to collect studies that would later be incorporated into publications such as *Common Sights in Town and Country Delineated and Described for Young Children,* a two-volume work he illustrated for the American Sunday School Union

in the 1850s. In light of Koellner's rambling over the continent, one of several trade cards he used to advertise his Philadelphia business can be considered truly autobiographical in its imagery (Fig. 32). Perhaps no other example of this period gives such an evocative variety of landscape views on a single trade card, or such an immediate record of the artist himself at work. The upper register contains a monumental architectural view and two pastoral landscape scenes. Below this we find a vignette to the left of the inscription that shows the artist at work in his studio, with classical busts in the background. On the right, the artist is shown sketching in nature. The bottom third of the card is taken up by an expansive landscape view along a coastline, with a locomotive

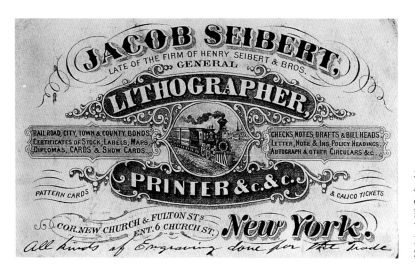

31. *Jacob Seibert, Lithographer, New York.* c. 1860. Jacob Seibert, lithographer. 3 x 5. The Warshaw Collection of Business Americana, Smithsonian Institution.

steaming away in the background. A comparison of the address on this card with those listed for him in the Philadelphia city directory indicates that this card was printed at the beginning of his career in America, some time between 1840 and 1844. It is a fitting introduction for a man who, although not well known today, spent so much of his life recording the American landscape in the lithographic medium.

Nowhere is the skill and ingenuity of lithographers in creating their own trade cards more amply demonstrated than in a card for the most important lithographer working in Philadelphia around midcentury, Peter S. Duval. When Duval came to Philadelphia from France in 1831, he was still in his twenties. He had both a consummate understanding of the lithographic trade and a firm belief in the power of advertising. His personal trade card from about 1840 (Fig. 33), executed by his highly skilled employee Albert Newsam, is a remarkable exercise in technical expertise and *trompe-l'oeil* illusionism. Like many of the storefront lithographs printed in Philadelphia during this period, this is a large card, measuring eleven by fourteen inches. The document at the upper right provides a key to the numerous other items arranged here. Under P. S. Duval's signature, we read that he "Execute[s] on Stone at the shortest notice all kinds of Drawings, Portraits, Landscapes, Historical Subjects, Animals etc. Also all kinds of Writings: Maps, Charts, Plans, professional and visitings Cards, Circulars, Billheads." Against the dark background of a tabletop Duval gives us a sample of each of these types of printing, all arranged around a central portrait of Alois Senefelder. On the right of the Senefelder portrait is a view of the Philadelphia Merchants' Exchange as seen from Duval's own building; on the left, a view of his establishment as seen from the Merchants' Exchange. Interestingly, in the lettering above and below the pictorial area, Duval imitated the appearance of engraving as one more proof of his firm's technical virtuosity in lithography. Duval advertised his business more heavily than any other lithographer in Philadelphia, and eagerly sought commissions from all over the country. On some of his later trade cards, Duval included Colorado mining scenes intended to appeal to the market for lithographic prints among customers in the Far West.[12]

In addition to his creativity in designing trade cards and other commercial advertising, Duval is important for having significantly advanced lithographic technology in the United States. Rumored at the time to have already the largest single lithographic business in America, in 1848 Duval began introducing steam power in his presses, the first Philadelphia lithographer to do so. More importantly, Duval is credited with being the first to introduce color lithography in American commercial printing on a large scale. While tinted or one-color lithographs had existed from an early stage, lithography in several colors was slow to develop, and it did so considerably earlier in Europe than in America. Alois Senefelder himself had briefly experimented with this problem, but it was not until about 1830 that lithography employing several colors was firmly

32. *Augustus Koellner, Engraver and Lithographer, Philadelphia.* c. 1840. Augustus Koellner, lithographer. $4^{3}/_{8}$ x $5^{1}/_{2}$. The New-York Historical Society.

33. *Peter S. Duval, Lithographer, Philadelphia.* c. 1840. Peter S. Duval, lithographer. 11 x 14. Historical Society of Pennsylvania.

established in Europe. In 1837, the French lithographer Godefroy Engelmann coined the word *chromolithographie* in a patent description, and it was not long before the term *chromolithograph,* or simply *chromo,* came to refer to lithographs executed in several colors. This process was much more complicated and time consuming than the black and white lithograph since each color had to be applied to the paper from a different stone. Because of the number of stones involved, it was also more expensive. For every print, each additional color had to be applied

with special care to insure proper registration without overlapping from one color zone to another. As Senefelder had predicted, most of the early European efforts were concerned with the reproduction of oil or watercolor paintings. It is generally held that the first chromolithograph produced in America was made in 1840 by the English immigrant William Sharp. Duval had printed tinted lithographs using one or two stones in the early 1840s, but the impetus for his production of true chromolithographs came when Duval procured the services of another immi-

grant craftsman, the Alsatian Christian Schuessele, in 1849. Shortly after his arrival in Philadelphia, the Duval company issued a flyer lithographed in color by Schuessele advertising itself as a "Lithographic and Color Printing Establishment" and claiming to be the first press to use steam power in its presses. The flyer also mentioned that the Duval firm would transfer wood blocks and copper or steel plates to lithographic stones.[13] This specialized service was the result of the experiments of Frederick Bourquin, Duval's Swiss shop foreman. In 1849, Bourquin went on to develop the process of zincography, whereby copper and steel engravings could be transferred to zinc plates rather than the more fragile and expensive lithographic stones.[14]

Although Duval and a few other lithographers

34. *Major and Knapp Lithographers, New York.*
1867. Major and Knapp, lithographers. 8³/₄ x 5¹/₂.
The Warshaw Collection of Business Americana,
Smithsonian Institution.

35. *Edward Chamberlin and Company, Boston.* 1860.
John H. Bufford, lithographer. 7¹/₂ x 5³/₄. The
New-York Historical Society.

the softness and subtlety obtained in the best chromolithography of the period. Here, as with many
other firms, Major and Knapp continued to advertise
themselves as both engravers and lithographers.
Trade cards in multiple colors for other patrons were
not common prior to the Civil War, unless one takes
into account the numerous clipper ship cards issued
in the major port cities. The fifties and sixties marked
the heyday of the clipper ship traffic to California,
and a great variety of these cards were issued,
although usually in small quantities. Sometimes carrying an illustration of the ships themselves, these
cards were also frequently characterized by the lively
patriotic imagery generated in the North during the
Civil War. The schedule of departures for the ship in
question was often indicated on the reverse of the
card. However, these cards were usually printed from
wood blocks, and the color, whether printed on or
applied by hand, was fairly crude. Such cards were
intended primarily for shipping agents rather than
the general public, and from the standpoint of distribution, they do not fit into the category of trade
cards in the usual sense of the term.[15]

Among the pioneers in introducing color lithography to trade cards in New England was the Bufford
Company of Boston. John H. Bufford trained initially with William S. Pendleton. According to most
sources, he then went to New York, where he
worked with Nathaniel Currier from 1835 to 1839,
after which he returned to Boston. However, this
seems at variance with information given on one of
Bufford's own trade cards in the New-York Historical Society collection, which gives the founding date

printed color trade cards for various firms in the early
1850s, most local tradesmen could more easily afford
engravings or black-and-white lithographs than such
sophisticated color work. Throughout the 1860s, the
most elaborate color trade cards tended to be those of
the lithographers themselves. A card from 1867 by
Major and Knapp (Fig. 34) is a beautiful example of

of his company as 1836. In any case, Bufford was back in Boston no later than 1840, and shortly thereafter began producing lithographs in color from multiple stones. His firm became increasingly prolific in the field of lithographic prints for framing and music-sheet covers. By the 1860s, Bufford also began to do a good deal of commercial work for advertising. A large card for Edward Chamberlin's Concentrated Leaven from 1860 (Fig. 35) is simple in composition, but is nevertheless a highly accomplished piece of chromolithography. Although somewhat limited in range, the colors are harmoniously balanced against the overall beige tone of the background. These colors are also skillfully gradated and dispersed over the entire card, rather than being concentrated in monolithic blocks as in the early stages of color lithograph printing. This card is important both as a superb specimen in full-color lithography and as an early example of the application of the trade card to the advertisement of a mass-marketed product, as opposed to strictly local businesses. The depiction of the black servant pointing out the wondrous qualities of Chamberlin's leavening to her mistress may seem to be a rather rude caricature, but as we shall see, it is quite mild in comparison to the images of blacks on trade cards after the Civil War. From this point, the Bufford company (known as Bufford and Sons after 1864) would be a leader in trade card printing in the northeast through the end of the century. However, after the death of John H. Bufford in 1870, the company would tend increasingly toward volume production and would never again show the kind of technical polish that it demonstrated in the sixties.

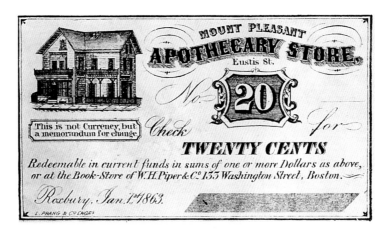

36. *Mount Pleasant Apothecary Store, Roxbury, Massachusetts.* 1863. Wood Engraving, Louis Prang and Company. 2^1/$_4$ x 3^7/$_8$. The New-York Historical Society.

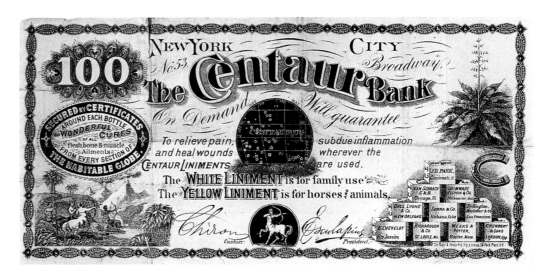

37. *Centaur Liniments.* c. 1865. Major and Knapp, lithographers. 2^7/$_8$ x 6^7/$_8$. The New-York Historical Society.

Despite the advances that had been made in color printing in the 1850s and 1860s, most lithographed trade cards continued to be printed in either black and white or a single color until well after the Civil War. Trade cards were still primarily a sideline for most major lithographic firms, which concentrated their efforts in color printing of landscape prints, reproductions of famous artworks, and other large lithographs. In this context, the direction taken by Louis Prang's company would have a revolutionary impact on the development of the trade card in the later nineteenth century. Prang was a German immigrant who arrived in New York in 1850. After a brief connection with Rosenthal and Duval in Philadelphia, Prang went to Boston, where, in 1856, he began a partnership with local lithographer Julius Mayer. Prang bought out Mayer in 1860, and despite the uncertain times, he prospered during the Civil War years by selling a variety of patriotic prints and maps to a public eager for documentary mementos of the war. In particular, he produced a series of card-size portraits of popular generals of the war, which reputedly sold in the millions at ten cents each.[16] This venture undoubtedly convinced Prang that considerable money was to be made in lithographed cards as well as in larger prints. In 1863, Prang published a series of album cards picturing American birds. These 2 3/4 by 4 1/2 inch cards were sold in sets and were intended to be collected in Prang's own patented hardcover albums. This specialty did not originate with Prang; several other British and American lithographers were by the 1860s also beginning to produce such cards for this increasingly popular nineteenth-cen-

38. *Prang's Aids for Object Teaching,* plate 5. 1874. Louis Prang and Company. Prints and Photographs Division, Library of Congress.

39. *Christmas Card.* 1876. Louis Prang and Co., lithographers. 3 1/8 x 5 5/8. Author's collection.

40. *Two Greeting Cards.* 1876. Louis Prang and Co., lithographers. 4¹/₄ x 2¹/₂ ea. Author's collection.

tury hobby. However, more than any other major American lithographer, Prang came to specialize in this aspect of the printing trade. In 1868, his house organ, *Prang's Chromo,* advertised envelopes of twelve album cards, grouped in twenty-six different categories, with certain categories including as many as nine different sets.[17] The subject matter consisted primarily of flowers, of birds and other animals, and of various landscape views. Each set of twelve was reasonably priced at fifty cents.

Louis Prang produced illustrated trade cards for local Boston merchants almost from the time he went into business there, but for several years they were exclusively in black and white, and many were engraved. One such card for a Roxbury apothecary, dating from 1863, takes the form of a certificate redeemable for twenty cents in trade (Fig. 36). Although they would be less popular after the 1870s, trade cards that imitated paper currency were relatively common, especially around the time of the Civil War. As can be seen in a black-and-white example for Centaur Liniments (Fig. 37), such cards were sometimes extremely elaborate. After the remarkable success of his album cards, Prang hit upon the idea of issuing relatively simple chromolithographed trade cards onto which the name of the advertiser could be stamped or overprinted later. Thus was begun the use of the so-called "stock" trade card, whereby a single card design could be adapted to the use of countless advertisers, each of whom could order from a number of designs continually turned out at Prang's large steam-powered printing plant. In *Prang's Aids for Object Teaching, Trades and Occupations,* published in 1874, one of the twelve color plates shows the typical activities of a lithographer's shop (Fig. 38). It is true that at the beginning of the 1870s, most lithographic printing continued to be done by hand-operated machinery, just as shown in this print. However, this is a far cry from the massive production facilities of Prang's plant, where apparently all work was being printed with steam-powered equipment by 1870.[18]

By his own account, Prang's first chro-

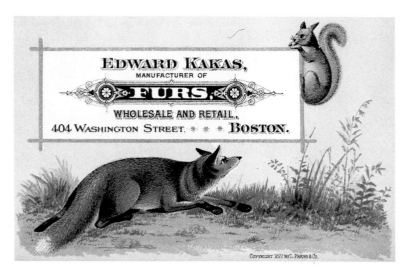

41. *Edward Kakas, Furrier, Boston.* 1877. Louis Prang and Co., lithographers. 2⅝ x 4¼. Author's collection.

42. *D. C. Stull, Milliner, Philadelphia.* 1876. Louis Prang and Co., lithographers. 2⅜ x 4. The Warshaw Collection of Business Americana, Smithsonian Institution.

molithographed trade cards bearing advertising were those he printed to publicize his exhibit at the Vienna International Exposition in 1873.[19] It was after he won a prize at this exposition that he began to copyright his card designs. In 1874, he opened a special agency in New York to market these "chromo cards." On the advice of a British friend, Prang also began placing Christmas and other holiday greetings in the blank spaces originally intended for advertisers. Christmas cards with floral subjects on a black background (Fig. 39) were introduced by Prang in 1875, and demand was so great that by the following year the Boston plant had trouble keeping up with orders for them. Thus Prang was almost singularly responsible for introducing not only the lithographed stock trade card, but, as a direct offshoot, the mass-produced holiday greeting card. Prang's multipurpose card designs frequently saw more use as greeting cards than they had initially as trade cards. One common example copyrighted in 1878 (Fig. 40) exists in various overprintings for commercial firms, but was more frequently used as a simple greeting card. The examples illustrated here are of the same dimensions as Prang's earlier album cards, are printed in a few bold colors, and usually have the bright red background which, along with the black, was characteristic of Prang cards of this period. Other designs seem to have been intended exclusively for trade cards. One example advertising a Boston furrier (Fig. 41), copyrighted 1877, also has a limited range of colors, but shows much finer detail than the earlier stock cards. The softness attained in the depiction of the animals contrasts nicely with the bold black lettering

The Mail Carrier of 100 years ago.

Catching and delivering the Fast Mails on the

LAKE SHORE & MICH. SOUTHERN RY.

The unrivaled Passenger Route.

NO FERRY TRANSFERS, NO DELAYS.

Secure Tickets by this popular thoroughfare.

M. F. ALLEN, Ag't, North Ferrisburg, Vt.

J. A. BURCH, Gen! East. Pass. Agt.   CHAS. PAINE, Gen! Sup!

See other side.

43. *Lake Shore and Michigan Southern Railway.* 1875. Clay, Cosack and Co., lithographers. 4¹/₂ x 3. The Warshaw Collection of Business Americana, Smithsonian Institution.

44. *Murphy Varnish Company, Newark.* c. 1880. Steel engraving. 2⁷/₈ x 4⁵/₈. Author's collection.

of the inset, which has the appearance of crisp engraving. Again, it is as if to suggest that in addition to its own obvious advantages, lithography could equal copper or steel plate engraving at its own game.

The Centennial Exhibition held in Philadelphia in 1876 provided an excellent opportunity for Prang and other commercial lithographers to display their wares, and, along with other businesses, to hand out free trade cards advertising their services. One Prang card prepared for the Philadelphia Exhibition describes on the reverse side his offering of over three hundred different designs for illustrated business, advertising, and visiting cards. Another Prang card elegantly displays the five major buildings of the exhibition against a black background with elegant floral detail (Fig. 42). This is a good example of the way in which the stock trade card was used; in this case it announces a grand opening by this advertiser during the exhibition. As with Prang's own cards, many of the trade cards prepared for this occasion were printed on both sides, with one side carrying the visual imagery and the other explaining the product. This fundamental departure from earlier practice went hand in hand with the trend toward much more liberal distribution of trade cards to the general public. As one example, Clay, Cosack and Company, another major lithography firm of Buffalo, New York, printed a standard "Centennial Business Card" picturing presidents Washington and Grant on the front. But in this case the back of the card, which features an advertisement for the Lake Shore and Michigan Southern Railway, is more fascinating in terms of Centennial-related imagery (Fig. 43).

While Prang and several other lithographers had produced a great variety of brilliantly colored trade

45. *Farmer, Livermore and Company, Engravers and Printers, Providence.* c. 1880. Steel engraving. 3¾ x 3. The Warshaw Collection of Business Americana, Smithsonian Institution.

46. *Clark's O. N. T. Thread.* 1872. Steel engraving, J. N. Allan, New York. 5 x 3⅜. The Warshaw Collection of Business Americana, Smithsonian Institution.

commercial printing throughout the century, particularly for the printing of bank notes, bonds, office forms, and business or calling cards. The delicacy possible in this medium can be seen in a fascinating business card printed for the agents of the Murphy Varnish Company (Fig. 44). The area at the top showing a chariot carrying a tank of Murphy's varnish is not much larger than a postage stamp—a mere 2¼ by 1¼ inches. Not unexpectedly, the most masterful steel-engraved cards were those issued to advertise the engravers themselves. The card for the engraving firm of Farmer, Livermore and Company (Fig. 45) features a female figure with the same forthright monumentality found on bank notes and bonds of the period.

A card from 1872 for Clark's "O. N. T." thread (Fig. 46) is an unusual example of an elaborate steel-engraved card commissioned for the purpose of advertising a specific product on a wide scale. The thread companies were among the first to begin nationwide distribution of trade cards, and the use of children in narrative situations such as this would be particularly frequent in the multitude of thread company trade cards issued in the later years of the century. This card unquestionably has a visual appeal quite independent of its commercial message, which is relegated to a secondary role. It was intended to be saved and collected in the family card album precisely because of the endearing genre quality of the image. Yet, as the overwhelming success of Prang's earlier, noncommercial album cards had demonstrated, color was the biggest attraction. At a time when color scarcely existed in periodical publishing, lithographic

cards by the late 1870s, it appears that even at that point, full-color trade cards were still more the exception than the rule. According to one source, a visitor to the Centennial Exhibition made an album of all the trade cards distributed there, and the resulting collection was eighty percent uncolored.[20] Many

exquisite black-and-white cards continued to be printed by engraving processes—specifically the more durable and refined process of steel engraving. Steel engraving remained an important medium for

47. *Clark's O. N. T. Thread.* 1878. Louis Prang and Co., lithographers. 2⅜ x 3⅝ ea. The Warshaw Collection of Business Americana, Smithsonian Institution.

printing in full color was still a novelty for the general public. Despite the fine detail of the steel-engraved trade card, it must have paled compared to the brilliant color of a series of ladies' pocket calendars that Prang printed for Clark's Thread in 1878 (Fig. 47). These diminutive cards are again characterized by Prang's red background and simple range of bright primary colors. (This formula had become so popular by that point that one of Prang's main competitors in Boston, the Bufford Company, had begun to imitate it.) By the beginning of the 1880s, trade cards lithographed in color had almost completely supplanted all kinds of engraved cards and were being distributed on an unprecedented scale by small firms and large industries alike. As more commercial lithographers began to specialize in this aspect of the trade, standards of quality became more competitive while prices for large orders steadily dropped. As production of the cards increased, so did the card craze of the public.

CHAPTER THREE

THE ADVERTISER
AND THE TRADE CARD

In the period following the Civil War, the essential catalyst that brought the products of rapidly expanding American industry together with the consumer was advertising of an unprecedented volume and diversity. If anything, the expansion of the advertising industry in the last third of the nineteenth century was even more dramatic than that of the economy in general. Between 1870 and 1900, the volume of American advertising increased by more than tenfold. Naturally, large increases in this field occurred in other industrialized nations as well, but nowhere, with the possible exception of Great Britain, did advertisers resort to such a multitude of media. American advertising in this period quickly developed a strategy aptly characterized by Daniel Boorstin as reflecting an aggressive, sometimes belligerent democracy, which "ruthlessly and relentlessly sought to widen the audience and to broaden its appeal."[1] In the cities, every available building and public conveyance was plastered with some sort of commercial message. In the countryside, enterprising advertisers easily convinced rural inhabitants to have the same thing done to their roadside farm buildings. Given such practices, a trade card for the New York Advertising Sign Company (Fig. 48), showing a sign painter daubing a message on Niagara Falls, is not so far from the truth. Certain advertisers indeed attempted to erect signs on the rapids below Niagara Falls during the 1880s, and one manufacturer went so far as to attempt painting an advertisement for his product on the Egyptian pyramids. As early as the mid–1870s, several states had begun to impose limitations to protect natural scenery from the onslaughts of hordes of sign painters, and some editorialists began to speak out for such limitations on a national scale.[2]

One of the major developments in post–Civil War advertising was the increasing use of newspapers and magazines. The effective exploitation of these media was due in part to the emergence of another phenomenon, the incorporated advertising agency. The first of these agencies was N. W. Ayer and Sons, founded in 1869, followed by the famous J. Walter Thompson Agency, founded in 1878. These agencies served as middlemen between advertisers and newspapers throughout the country. However, in the late 1880s, general advertising agencies still conducted most of their business with only about one-tenth, or roughly fifteen hundred, of the nation's newspapers.[3] With the possible exception of the highly aggressive patent medicine trade, most of the limited advertising in small-town newspapers continued to be placed by local merchants. The so-called country weeklies, rural equivalents of city daily newspapers, also carried large amounts of patent medicine advertising. In the case of the nationally distributed monthly magazines, advertising began to appear on a regular basis at the beginning of the 1860s, but for many years very few pages of any given issue would be devoted to advertisements. As late as 1880, advertising pages were almost invariably divided among several advertisers, with the arrangement of the advertisements varying little from week to week or month to month. Full-page advertisements for a single product were almost unheard of. Some of the more popular monthly magazines even showed a distinct reluctance to permit extensive outside advertising. For years, most of the advertising space in *Harper's Monthly* was reserved for the firm's own book-publishing business. When the Howe Sewing Machine Company offered eighteen thousand dollars for a full page in *Harper's Monthly* in the early seventies, they were

48. *The New York Advertising Sign Company.* c. 1885. Donaldson Brothers, lithographers. $2^{7/8}$ x $4^{5/8}$. The New-York Historical Society.

might include an illustration of the product being advertised, as was particularly common for appliances like stoves or sewing machines. Also, the reverse might have a space set aside for the local dealer of the product to be printed in later, as seen on the back of a card for the widely advertised Mrs. Potts' Cold Handle Sad Iron (Fig. 49). In the case of the stock cards made for the use of widely varying trades, the reverse side sometimes provides the only indication of the business that ultimately distributed a particular card. When the front advertised one specific product, a company might use the back of the card to mention one or more other products. The front of one patent medicine trade card carries an illustration advertising Mother Swan's Worm Syrup; on the back, the E. S. Wells Company took the opportunity to advertise several additional items in its line, ranging from corn plasters to rat poison (Fig. 50). Here the arrangement of the messages and illustrations closely resembles a block of small magazine advertisements; like many purveyors of patent medicines, the Wells Company advertised heavily in periodicals as well. Occasionally, the information on the back of the card was printed in a language other than English, in order to target local immigrant concentrations such as Germans or Scandinavians in the Midwest, or for distribution in a foreign country where the product might have been marketed. There are even some cases in which patent medicine makers and other high-volume advertisers printed the message on the back of the card in three or more different languages.

Other major differences between the poster and

politely refused.[4] While the number of pages given over to black-and-white advertisements progressively increased in the 1880s, color advertising in magazines was still almost nonexistent. The *Galaxy,* which had been one of the first to accept large quantities of "miscellaneous" advertising, experimented with color inserts for certain advertisers between 1868 and 1870, but no other major magazines followed its lead, and the *Galaxy* itself soon ceased this practice.[5] Thus, even though the rates charged by the major magazines dropped as circulation increased, the opportunities for illustration available to advertisers in these magazines were still very limited in the 1880s.

The two advertising media that proliferated most dramatically in the post–Civil War years were the illustrated poster and the trade card. Both became more reasonably priced and accessible to advertisers as lithographic technology itself rapidly improved in the seventies and eighties. However, while equally colorful and direct in its visual imagery, the trade card differed fundamentally from the poster in its method of conveying the advertising message. By 1880, most trade cards were printed on both sides, and while the back side of the cards obviously meant nothing once the cards were pasted into family albums, that side's use must be duly considered in assessing the strategies of late-nineteenth-century advertising. Almost always printed in black and white, the reverse side often provided an extensive description of the product. If it was not already shown on the front, this side

49. *Mrs. Potts' Cold Handle Sad Irons.* c. 1880. Lithograph (reverse side). 3 x 4¼. Author's collection.

50. *Mother Swan's Worm Syrup.* c. 1885. Lithograph (reverse side). 4¾ x 3⅛. The New-York Historical Society.

the trade card as advertising media are that trade cards proliferated into even the most remote communities and were used in one way or another by all kinds of tradesmen and merchants, however modest their businesses might be. As Louis Prang said, "Hardly a business man in the country has not at one time or another made use of such cards to advertize his wares."[6] The extraordinarily wide use of the trade card in the late nineteenth century can be largely explained by its extremely low cost and availability to the advertiser. The gradual replacement of lithographic stones by cheaper and more durable zinc plates, along with the increasing use of steam in printing plants, greatly expanded lithographic production while at the same time reducing prices. In the early 1870s, Prang had dominated the market in stock trade card printing, but by the end of the decade so many new commercial lithography firms had emerged that the competition, especially in New York City, was ferocious. Cards distributed by these lithographers to promote their own businesses emphasized not only their services and facilities (almost all made a point of their steam-powered plants), but also their competitive prices. Symptomatic of this competition, the Donaldson Brothers Company, which was one of the giants in trade card production in the eighties, issued a calendar trade card in 1878 that mentioned on the back "prices to suit the times."

In terms of sheer numbers, stock cards, onto which any number of business names and addresses could be overprinted, were by far the most common in the later nineteenth century, and although gener-

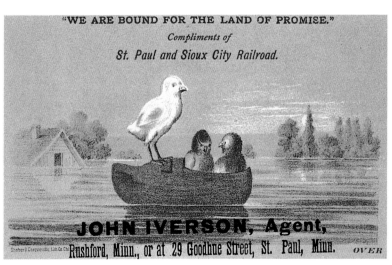

51. *Edmund Whitehead, Butcher, Fall River, Massachusetts* (2³/₄ x 4³/₈) and *St. Paul and Sioux City Railroad* (2⁷/₈ x 4¹/₄). c. 1885. Shober and Carqueville, lithographers. Author's collection.

ally less interesting than those custom printed for specific businesses, they were also much less expensive. Here, the price depended on whether the patron's name was to be printed on by the lithographer. One New York company advertised one thousand cards at twelve dollars with the trade printed in, seven dollars without. Another New York firm issued a sample stock card, which it offered to print for as little as $3.25 a thousand. Regardless of where it was printed, a single stock card might have been used to advertise any number of different and geographically separated businesses. A simple card in two colors printed by Shober and Carqueville of Chi-

cago, one of ten in their "Landseer Card Series," was used to publicize interests as diverse as Edmund Whitehead's butcher shop in Fall River, Massachusetts, and a railroad agent in Minnesota (Fig. 51). The latter extolled at length the opportunities for prospective settlers in that state on the reverse of the card. The ubiquity of simple colored stock cards such as these is reflected in the several instances in which they are pictured along with photographs and other mundane objects in still-life paintings of the later nineteenth century, particularly in the peculiar American genre of "bachelor's shelf" and office board still-life.[7]

Prior to the 1870s, Currier and Ives had built their reputation almost exclusively on large, hand-colored lithographic prints intended for the parlor walls of American households. Perhaps inspired in part by the success of Louis Prang, Currier and Ives began producing a line of stock trade cards in the later seventies as well. Aside from a few for tobacco companies, almost none of their cards were actually designed for specific patrons, and again we find that a single card design often served a vast array of businesses. Many of these designs were actually newly copyrighted reissues of earlier Currier and Ives prints, printed on a much smaller scale. Most Currier and Ives trade cards

This Class, as well as the Heaviest Draft Horses, use the LION HARNESS AND REIN LEATHERS. Manufactured only by C. C. WARREN, Waterbury, Vt.

LION TRADE MARK C.C.WARREN

EDWIN THORNE. Record 2:16½.

52. *C. C. Warren Leathergoods, Waterbury, Vermont.* 1882. Currier and Ives, lithographers. 3⅜ x 5⅛. Author's collection.

fit into one of two principal categories, the comic series and the race horse series. The race horse cards, most of which showed famous trotters of the period, were usually taken directly from among their variety of larger prints that pictured horses of one kind or another. Burdick lists over thirty different Currier and Ives trade card issues featuring famous racing champions of the period.[8] Despite their considerably smaller scale, these cards retain much of the character of the larger works on which they were based; even the simple printed colors recall the broad hand-tinting typical of the original prints (Fig. 52). Currier and Ives comic cards were more robust in their caricatural imagery, but these also frequently centered around the life of the racetrack. While all of these were stock cards, they were often used to advertise nationally marketed products in the early eighties. Several designs copyrighted in 1880 were overprinted with the trademark of the Clark Thread Company, the same firm for which Prang had produced several custom-designed cards in the later 1870s (Fig. 53). Because of their substantial reputation in larger popular prints, Currier and Ives already had an enthusiastic audience, which perhaps explains why they were able to charge higher prices for their cards than most of their competition.[9] Yet compared to most other trade card printers, their output seems to have been small and was generally confined to the early 1880s, before the real heyday of the custom-printed cards produced by the larger commercial lithographers. Thus, even though both the race horse and comic themes were often imitated by other printers, cards by Currier and Ives are quite rare today.

While most stock cards for local businesses were mass produced by the big lithographic houses in eastern cities, one can occasionally come across some crudely printed and quite curious cards from more isolated areas dating from late in the nineteenth century. One example, an uncolored, engraved card advertising a general store in Hanover, Kansas (Fig. 54), tells us little enough about the merchant, and there is no indication as to the printer. Since cards such as this had neither the color nor the sophisticated illustration of the stock cards manufactured by major lithographic printers, they were less likely to be saved, and are thus all the more ephemeral. Likewise, some cards produced for widely advertised products were so primitive in imagery and execution that they might be categorized as genuinely naive art in much the same sense as many American paintings of the period. One particularly striking example is an uncolored lithographic card for Muzzy's Sun Gloss Starch (Fig. 55). By comparison to most, this card seems clumsy and hesitant in its rendering; yet, while there is no indication of the designer or printer, there is a highly personal quality to the illustration that was usually lacking in the more sophisticated designs of the larger lithographic companies. However, by the 1880s, the quaint simplicity of the illustration on the Muzzy's Starch card was much more the exception than the rule. Public expectations in terms of both color and lively imagery were much higher, and

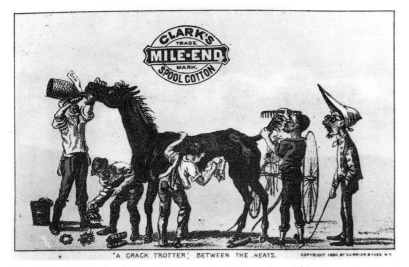 

"A CRACK TROTTER" BETWEEN THE HEATS. COPYRIGHT 1880, BY CURRIER & IVES N.Y.

"A CRACK TROTTER" IN THE HARNESS OF THE PERIOD. COPYRIGHT 1880, BY CURRIER & IVES N.Y.

53. *Clark's Mile-End Thread.* 1880. Currier and Ives, lithographers. Each 3¼ x 5. Rare Books and Manuscripts Division, The New York Public Library. Astor, Lenox and Tilden Foundations.

advertisers, aided by the sophisticated production methods of the lithographic industry, were more than willing to flood the consumer market with exactly what it wanted.

The custom-printed or private trade card, commissioned by a specific manufacturer or merchandiser to advertise its business, was distributed to the public in several ways. In the larger eastern cities, and particularly in New York, the large retail department stores that had developed so rapidly in the years after the Civil War were becoming increasingly competitive. Many gave out individualized trade cards, often with holiday greetings or calendars on the reverse. Some

manufactured goods, especially products like coffee, soap, and processed foods, came with trade cards included in the packages (in the latter case, this practice was generally rare until factory-packaged foodstuffs became more common toward the end of the century). The back of one card for the Jersey Coffee Company points out that it is one of a hundred in their series of photographic views. Even considering the company's claim that there were no two cards alike in any case of their coffee, the accumulation of an entire set must have been a daunting task. By far the most common means of distributing trade cards was through smaller retailers, and it is precisely for

this reason that so many cards filtered down to even the most remote towns and villages. Earlier in the century, general store owners had been relatively independent in that they had purchased bulk goods from the wholesale house of their choice, with brand names being of little consequence. As brand-name recognition became a distinct strategy of advertising in the last decades of the century, manufacturers were eager to supply the local merchant with whatever advertising materials he might agree to use in dealing with his customers. Large quantities of trade cards advertising specific products were usually distributed directly to the retailers through "drummers," the

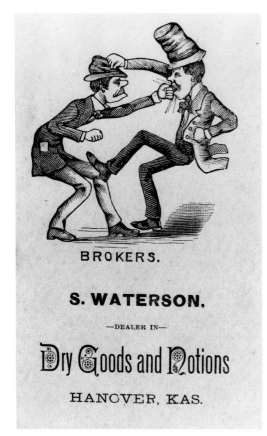

BROKERS.

S. WATERSON,

—DEALER IN—

Dry Goods and Notions

HANOVER, KAS.

54. *S. Waterson, Drygoods, Hanover, Kansas.* c. 1890. Anonymous wood engraving with metal type. 4³/₈ x 2⁵/₈. Author's collection.

55. *Muzzy's Sun Gloss Starch.* c. 1880. Lithograph. 4¹/₂ x 3. Author's collection.

commercial agents who ranged over the country as intermediaries between manufacturers and retail outlets. The generous supply of chromolithographed trade cards and other advertising materials was in fact a powerful incentive for the general store owner to

agree to stock the product in question. A striking example of this practice can be found in the message on the back of a card for Dr. Radcliffe's Great Remedy, which was clearly intended for the retailer rather than the customer. With the first order, the company promised to send, along with a free pocket watch, "a good supply of Chromos [trade cards like this one], Bills, Posters, etc., an abundance of each sufficient to scatter broadcast all over your county, and have it generally known that you are the agent."

While the nineteenth-century family certainly had much less choice in the way of foods, recreational goods, and other consumer items than is available today, the range of household necessities advertised on nineteenth-century trade cards is perhaps not so different from today as one might expect. In a few major categories, however, there is a striking difference between the mass-media campaigns of today and the limited efforts of one hundred years ago. This is most evident in the case of alcoholic beverages. In the later nineteenth century, a much higher percentage of Americans maintained strong moral objections to drinking than they do today. Therefore, it is not surprising to find that advertising for beers, wines, and spirits was almost universally banned by the publishers of popular magazines. Likewise, in a medium as family oriented as trade cards, promotion of alcoholic beverages was extremely rare. Most advertising for beers and spirits was to be found in the taverns and saloons where they were most commonly consumed, in the form of colorful and often rather suggestive posters and store cards. Thus while the brewers and distillers provided considerable business

RIDING
SIDE SADDLE

56. *American Tobacco Company.* c. 1895.
Lithograph. 4¹/₈ x 2¹/₂. Author's collection.

for lithographers in work of a larger scale, they did not play any considerable role in the history of trade cards.

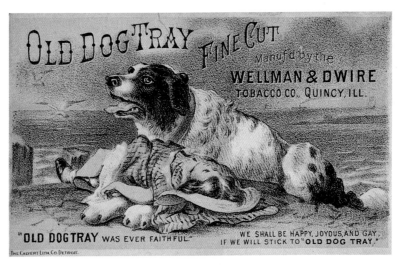

OLD DOG TRAY FINE CUT
Manuf'd by the
WELLMAN & DWIRE
TOBACCO CO., QUINCY, ILL.

"OLD DOG TRAY WAS EVER FAITHFUL."

WE SHALL BE HAPPY, JOYOUS, AND GAY,
IF WE WILL STICK TO "OLD DOG TRAY."

THE CALVERT LITH. CO. DETROIT.

57. *Old Dog Tray (Wellman and Dwire Tobacco Company).* c. 1885. Calvert Lithography Company, lithographers. 3¹/₈ x 5. Author's collection.

Trade cards for tobacco are somewhat more common than those for beer and liquor, but still represent a relatively insignificant percentage of the total output. This is not so much due to moral objections as to the fact that at least in the case of cigarettes, the manufacturers had a built-in alternative in the form of the cigarette card. The true cigarette card has a history of its own, which need not be considered in detail here. Cigarette cards were usually smaller and on heavier stock than trade cards. They were sometimes referred to as "stiffeners" because, in addition to attracting the customers, they gave further support to the package. Generally, cigarette cards were less popular in America than in England, where they continued to be placed in packages and enthusiastically collected throughout the early twentieth century. Like posters for alcoholic beverages, American cigarette cards of the nineteenth century often reflect the predominantly male audience for which they were intended. Many carried illustrations of buxom burlesque performers such as the dainty bit of cheesecake shown on a card for the American Tobacco Company of Baltimore (Fig. 56). When tobacco products were advertised on trade cards, the imagery employed was often completely unrelated to the product. In many cases, the illustrations make a passing reference to the brand names, which were myriad and sometimes quite bizarre. The poignant scene on a card for Old Dog Tray tobacco (Fig. 57) provides a sharp contrast to the racy nature of most true cigarette cards.

58. *Madame Monand's Tan Remover.* c. 1865.
Lithograph and metal type with hand-applied
color. 5 x 3⅛. The Warshaw Collection of
Business Americana, Smithsonian Institution.

59. *Barry's Tricopherous Hair Tonic.* c. 1885.
Lithograph. 5¼ x 3. The Warshaw Collection of
Business Americana, Smithsonian Institution.

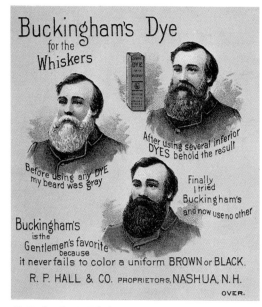

60. *Buckingham's Whisker Dye.* c. 1880.
Lithograph. 3½ x 3. Author's collection.

Another field of products that was advertised
much less extensively in the nineteenth century than
in our own is cosmetics. Again, much of the explana-
tion lies in the social and moral reservations about
their use. Here, however, attitudes seem to have varied considerably over the decades. During the early
Republic, cosmetics had negative associations with
aristocracy. Then, in the fifties and sixties, the vogue
for Parisian fashions resulted in even the most respect-
able women using facial make-up. Finally, the seventies and eighties brought a moralistic reversal that

branded "painted" women as being of dubious moral repute, if not outright prostitutes.[10] Preparations to preserve or restore the complexion were often home-made rather than purchased. Whatever preparations they might have used in private, American women of the late nineteenth century were expected to look as natural as possible in public. Judging from the costume and elaborate applied color, a trade card for Madame Monand's complexion treatment (Fig. 58) probably dates from around the time of the Civil War. The name of the product itself reinforces the association of cosmetics with French stylishness. While concoctions that were meant to remove blemishes or facial hair did not have the same stigma attached to them as cosmetics worn in public, none of these products are common on trade cards. The only exception to the general tendency regarding the advertising of cosmetics was hair preparations, which appear fairly frequently on trade cards. The popularity of hair tonics and restoratives was undoubtedly due in large part to the fact that in the later nineteenth century, fashion demanded much longer hair of women, which was itself another emblem of the "natural" female. Period photographs confirm that the length of the woman's tresses on a card for Barry's Tricopherous Hair Tonic (Fig. 59) was hardly exceptional. Likewise, in an age when most men sported mustaches or beards in one configuration or another, preparations such as Buckingham's Whisker Dye (Fig. 60) strongly appealed to masculine vanity.

The vast majority of trade cards printed in the late nineteenth century were for common household items that most families purchased at one time or

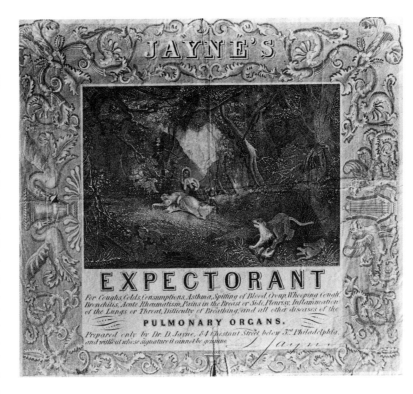

61. *Jayne's Expectorant.* 1847. Engraving. 6¼ x 7. The New-York Historical Society.

another. Among these, patent medicine businesses, which were also the heaviest advertisers in periodicals,[11] made up the largest single category of card distributors. The advertising expenditures for proprietary medicines were enormous, amounting to 30 or even 40 percent of the gross sales of the product.[12] Such expenditures can be explained not only by the intense competition among patent medicine companies, but also by the huge profits that could be made. In a society where physicians were inaccessible to some and mistrusted by many, Americans were particularly inclined toward doctoring themselves, whether the medicines they purchased were of any real benefit or not. Even though substantial advances were being made in the study of infectious diseases, general ignorance of the role of bacteria in transmit-

62. *Mustang Liniment.* c. 1885. Schumacher and Ettlinger, lithographers. 3 x 4½. Rare Books and Manuscripts Division, The New York Public Library. Astor, Lenox and Tilden Foundations.

63. *Merchant's Gargling Oil.* c. 1885. Courier Lithographic Co., lithographers. 4½ x 3. Rare Books and Manuscripts Division, The New York Public Library. Astor, Lenox and Tilden Foundations.

ting disease, combined with poor diet, rendered the population vulnerable to many diseases that are virtually unknown in twentieth-century America. As late as 1900, influenza, tuberculosis, and gastrointestinal ailments remained, in that order, the three biggest killers. Major typhoid epidemics continued to occur even after the turn of the century.[13] Given the general state of health care in the nineteenth century, it is not surprising that some patent medicine makers would unscrupulously exploit public credulity. Sales boomed all the more as the result of the lingering wounds and diseases that afflicted veterans following the Civil War. Despite widespread abuses,

federal regulations governing the contents of proprietary medicines were not enacted until 1906, and since the makers jealously guarded the "secrets" of their remedies, the consumer's choice of what to buy, as well as the retailer's choice of what to stock on his shelves, was largely dictated by intensive advertising.

Patent medicine companies were among the first to use trade cards on a wide scale. An especially early example, copyrighted 1847, is a large card on thin paper advertising Jayne's Expectorant (Fig. 61). David Jayne was a legitimate physician who had practiced in New Jersey before moving to Philadelphia to establish his drug business. Although subsequently

LYDIA E. PINKHAM'S
VEGETABLE COMPOUND
IS A POSITIVE CURE
*For all those painful Complaints and Weaknesses
so common to our best female population.*

It will cure entirely the worst form of Female Complaints, all Ovarian troubles, Inflammation, Ulceration, Falling and Displacements of the Womb and the consequent Spinal Weakness, and is particularly adapted to the Change of Life.

It will dissolve and expel Tumors from the uterus in an early stage of development. The tendency to cancerous humors there is checked very speedily by its use. It removes faintness, flatulency, destroys all craving for stimulants, and relieves weakness of the stomach. It cures Bloating, Headaches, Nervous Prostration, General Debility, Sleeplessness, Depression and Indigestion.

That feeling of bearing down, causing pain, weight and backache is always permanently cured by its use.

It will at all times and under all circumstances act in harmony with the laws that govern the female system. For the cure of Kidney Complaints of either sex, this Compound is unsurpassed.

LYDIA E. PINKHAM'S VEGETABLE COMPOUND is prepared at 233 and 235 Western Avenue, Lynn, Mass. Price, $1.00. Six bottles for $5.00. Sent by mail in the form of pills, also in the form of lozenges, on receipt of price, $1.00 per box, for either. Send for pamphlet. All letters of inquiry promptly answered. Address as above.

No family should be without *LYDIA E. PINKHAM'S LIVER PILLS.* They cure constipation, biliousness, and torpidity of the liver, 25c. per box

Sold by all Druggists.

COMPLIMENTS OF

64. *Lydia E. Pinkham's Vegetable Compound.*
c. 1880. Lithograph (reverse side). 4$^{1}/_{8}$ x 2$^{5}/_{8}$.
Author's collection.

65. *Mrs. Winslow's Soothing Syrup.* 1887. J. Ottmann, lithographers. 3$^{1}/_{4}$ x 5. Author's collection.

shunned by the medical profession, Jayne amassed millions over a thirty-year period through relentless marketing of his curatives. He was eventually charged with attempting to bribe his way into the United States Senate, an apparently groundless accusation.[14] As would frequently be the case with later cards, the dramatic scene taking place on Jayne's rather primitively printed card has nothing to do with the product itself. If it was anything like Jayne's later medicines, this product probably contained both alcohol and opiates. Typically, the card lists a host of ailments that can be cured by this medicine but gives no indication as to the ingredients. Many patent medicines were advertised as having even broader

applications; in some cases, they were literally described as being equally beneficial for human or veterinary treatment, as seen on a delightful card on a circus theme for Mustang Liniment (Fig. 62). A card for Merchant's Gargling Oil (Fig. 63) satirizes the ongoing controversy surrounding Darwin's theory of evolution by showing an ape claiming that if the ointment was good for man and beast, it should be doubly good for him.

The freedom from restraints that would have been imposed in much periodical advertising made the trade card an ideal advertising medium for patent medicines. It allowed the advertiser to make whatever claims he wished, no matter how rambling or

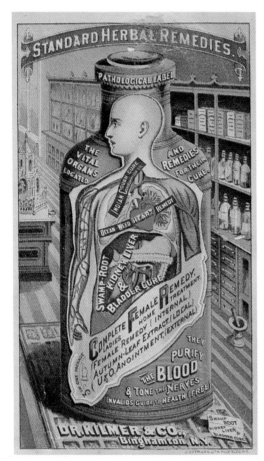

66. *Dr. Kilmer and Company Standard Herbal Remedies.* c. 1885. J. Ottmann, lithographers. 5⅛ x 3. The New-York Historical Society.

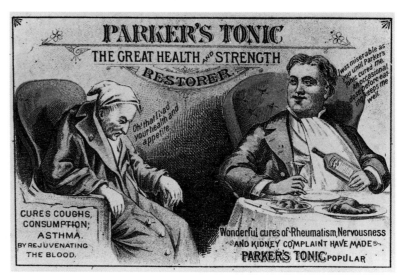

67. *Parker's Tonic.* c. 1885. Lithograph. 3 x 4¼. The Warshaw Collection of Business Americana, Smithsonian Institution.

outlandish those claims might be. Lydia Pinkham's Vegetable Compound was one of the most popular remedies of the later nineteenth century, and was still widely marketed well into the twentieth. One of the reasons for the popularity of this product was the range of "women's complaints" and other disorders it allegedly cured. The back of one card (Fig. 64) goes into great detail about the astonishing curative powers of Pinkham's famous concoction. The very real dangers of remedies such as this are evident in the claim that use of this medicine would cure and even prevent cancer. Despite its innocuous name, Pinkham's Compound contained over 20 percent alcohol. A number of other patent medicines contained considerably more; Balm of Gilead, which was

endorsed by a number of "retired clergymen," was 70 percent alcohol.[15] Endorsements, whether by clergymen, social and political celebrities, or ordinary consumers, were a major component in the advertising of patent medicine makers and were often featured on the back of their trade cards. On an attractively printed card for Mrs. Winslow's Soothing Syrup dating from 1887 (Fig. 65), a mother dangles a tempting vial of the syrup over her baby. Aside from its teething miseries, perhaps part of the reason the infant seems so anxious to have it is that Winslow's Syrup contained a large amount of morphia. Over three-fourths of a million bottles were sold annually in the United States, even though it was frequently cited in medical journals as the cause

ADMINISTERING
THE NORWEGIAN BALM
FOR
CATARRH.

Ask Your Druggist For it.
N. B. Phelps, Prop'r
No. 6 Murray St, New York.

68. *Norwegian Balm.* c. 1885. Lithograph.
$5^{1}/_{2}$ x $3^{3}/_{8}$. The New-York Historical Society.

DR. SCOTT'S ELECTRIC CORSET.

DR. SCOTT'S ELECTRIC HAIR-BRUSH.

DR. SCOTT'S ELECTRIC HAIR-CURLER.

DR. SCOTT'S ELECTRIC TOOTH-BRUSH.

69. *Dr. Scott's Electrical Products.* c. 1890.
Lithograph. 6 x $4^{1}/_{4}$. The Warshaw Collection of
Business Americana, Smithsonian Institution.

of fatal opiate poisoning.[16] Many consumers who were otherwise enthusiastic champions of prohibition undoubtedly found comfort, if not a genuine cure, in a host of alcohol-laden tonics and bitters. With the remedies that also contained opiates, as many did, the risk of long-term dependence was all the more profound.

While the illustrations on patent medicine trade cards often had little or nothing to do with the product, the imagery used in advertising some curatives could also be surprisingly explicit. In an apparent attempt at scientific legitimacy, a bizarre card for Dr. Kilmer's line of remedies (Fig. 66) shows the various organs upon which they purportedly worked their benefits. On a card for Parker's Tonic (Fig. 67), the contrast between a haggard, emaciated sufferer and his well-fed counterpart at the dinner table reflects the popular misconception about the relationship between physical robustness and health. Children and adults alike were considered well according to the extent of their appetites, and loss of appetite, along with many more serious maladies, was often attributed to some unspecified imbalance or impurity of the blood. Nineteenth-century Americans routinely dosed themselves with purifying tonics, especially in the spring, when blood was considered to be particularly impure after the long months of winter. For more simple ailments, imaginative purveyors could always base their appeal on the apparatus by which their curative was administered, as shown in the curious manner in which one lady makes use of Norwegian Balm (Fig. 68).

An even more blatant form of quackery was the use of electricity as a restorative and blood purifier. Throughout the late nineteenth century, any number of mystifying and often dangerous devices were marketed by unscrupulous entrepreneurs. One of the most widely advertised items of this sort was Dr. Scott's Electric Brush, which claimed to cure as many nervous and organic disorders as any tonic. One of

70. *Magnetized Food Company.* 1882. Hatch Company, lithographers. 4³/₈ x 3¹/₄. The New-York Historical Society.

Dr. Scott's trade cards indicates that electric corsets, toothbrushes, and haircurlers were also available (Fig. 69). The comely female figure was obviously meant to suggest the additional cosmetic benefits of Scott's products. One company even marketed a medicinal food that owed its supposed curative powers to the fact that it was "vitalized" by magne-tism. Appropriately enough, the trade card for Magnetized Food was in the shape of a magnet (Fig. 70).

After patent medicines, perhaps the next most frequently encountered product on trade cards is thread. This may at first seem curious, but it must be remembered that throughout the nineteenth century, most family clothing was made in the home rather than purchased in stores. Until at least midcentury, the majority of factory-produced clothing consisted of crudely made work clothes. Production of ready-made clothing increased dramatically in the last third of the nineteenth century, from about 187 millions of dollars worth in 1869 to 772 millions in 1899,[17] but most of this production consisted of undergarments, hats, and men's suits. Ordinary clothing for daily wear, and especially women's and children's clothing, was still largely produced by women sewing for their own families. For most married women, sewing thread was as much a staple as sugar or flour. The thread market in America was dominated by a handful of fiercely competitive companies. Earlier in the century, the British had supplied most of the thread for the American market. The demand for their product was so great that J. and P. Coats and William Barbour and Sons both established thread works in America after the Civil War. By this point, several American manufacturers had entered the market. The back of one Willimantic Thread trade card from the late 1870s referred to its product as "superior to that of British manufacture," reflecting the keen competition between native and foreign thread manufacturers for the rapidly growing American market. All of these companies advertised extensively, but were perhaps unique in that they used the trade card more than any other advertising medium.

No other category of trade cards mentioned so little about the actual product, and none took such flights of fantasy, as did those of the thread manufacturers. Since one spool of thread looks more or less like any other, the thread makers relied primarily on consumer recognition of the name and the trademark printed on the label at the end of the spool. Thus the spool was frequently represented on the trade card, and often in quite ingenious ways. As we have seen, the Clark Thread Company had been an early patron of both Prang and Currier and Ives in the 1870s. During the eighties and nineties, an enormous variety of trade cards was issued for Clark's O. N. T. and Mile End brands, many of which show an unusually high quality of printing. A colorful card on a circus clown theme brings the company spool label into the picture with great animation (Fig. 71). Another Clark's card is actually in the shape of a spool of thread (Fig. 72). The domesticity of the scene, typical of many threadmakers' cards, is reinforced here by the slogan at the bottom of the card: "Nothing stronger can there be, but mother's love and O. N. T." If the thread manufacturers made any allusion to the intrinsic qualities of their product, it was usually in reference to its strength. Along with a number of other advertisers, the thread companies were quick to exploit the sensation created over P. T. Barnum's purchase of Jumbo, supposedly the largest elephant in captivity, which he transported to America in 1882.[18] Willimantic was only one of several brands of thread with trade cards from the early eighties on which

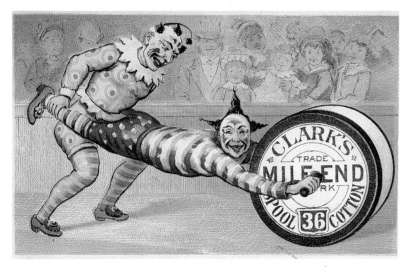

71. *Clark's Mile-End Thread.* c. 1885. Lithograph. 3 x 4½. The Warshaw Collection of Business Americana, Smithsonian Institution.

72. *Clark's O. N. T. Thread.* c. 1885. Lithograph. 4½ x 2⅞. Author's collection.

Jumbo was ensnared, hoisted, or dragged (Fig. 73). Even more fanciful is the card for the Merrick Company showing a train traversing a river on a railway of Merrick's six-cord thread (Fig. 74).

A factor closely related to thread manufacturing was the increasing importance of the sewing machine in the later nineteenth century. It is likely that no other appliance had such an impact on both a major industry and the household. In the period between its invention by Elias Howe in 1844 and the Civil War, an enormous number of new patents for sewing machines were developed in the United States. By the end of the century, over two hundred sewing machine companies had appeared, some by developing new patents, some by infringing on the patents of oth-ers.[19] Most of these companies were short-lived, lasting ten years or less. Others only manufactured specialized machines for industrial use, many of which were exported. However, the largest and most profitable companies aimed primarily at the family market, and it soon became clear that the sewing machine would have its most profound impact within the home. As early as 1858, an article in *National Magazine* applauded the benefit of the sewing machine for the professional seamstress, but also noted that "the great source of demand is now for family use, and the time is not far distant when a sewing machine will be deemed an essential piece of furniture in every well-ordered household."[20] An idea of just how significant the sewing machine could be in making clothing in the home is reflected in the estimate by one sewing machine company that a man's shirt required about fourteen hours of hand sewing, as opposed to just over an hour on a machine.[21]

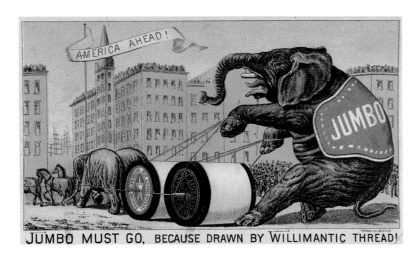

JUMBO MUST GO, BECAUSE DRAWN BY WILLIMANTIC THREAD!

73. *Willimantic Thread.* c. 1883. Forbes Company, lithographers. 3 x 4³/₄. Rare Books and Manuscripts Division, The New York Public Library. Astor, Lenox and Tilden Foundations.

74. *Merrick Thread.* c. 1885. Dando Printing and Publishing Company, lithographers. 4¹/₄ x 3. The Warshaw Collection of Business Americana, Smithsonian Institution.

Among the five largest sewing machine manufacturers, the Singer Company and Wheeler and Wilson appeared first, in the early 1850s. They were followed by Domestic, in 1869, and the New Home and White companies, established in 1876. With the exception of Wheeler and Wilson, which was absorbed by Singer, all survive in some form to this day. These firms all advertised heavily in women's magazines and other periodical literature, but also issued a great many trade cards. Sometimes costing almost one hundred dollars, sewing machines represented a substantial investment and could not be afforded by everyone. Still, advertisers attempted to convince women that the sewing machine was a household necessity. It was represented as the fondest dream of the young maiden, and even as a precondition for marriage (Fig. 75). The sewing machine was also portrayed as a luxurious and prestigious piece of furniture that could beautify the home, both by producing decorative furnishings and by its very presence in the parlor (Fig. 76). Together with complicated paper patterns and models illustrated in the fashion plates of women's magazines, the sewing machine provided the means to make clothing with the elaborate embroidery and other detail that was so much in vogue in women's fashions of the late nineteenth century. This tendency toward fancy embellishment of homemade apparel was so pervasive that one dress-reform activist openly criticized women who, because of their vanity, were enslaved by their sewing to the point that they denied themselves wholesome outdoor exercise.[22]

Another group of manufactured goods that appears with great frequency on trade cards is soaps and cleansers. Unlike most household staples, this field did not really develop until well into the nineteenth century. Soap had traditionally been made at home and was frequently used as barter for other

75. *Domestic Sewing Machine Company.* c. 1885. Lithograph. 3 x 4¾. Rare Books and Manuscripts Division, The New York Public Library. Astor, Lenox and Tilden Foundations.

76. *White Sewing Machine Company.* c. 1880. W. J. Morgan and Company, lithographers. 4¾ x 3. The Warshaw Collection of Business Americana, Smithsonian Institution.

goods in country stores. Even in the early twentieth century, soapmaking remained common in many American households. Initially, commercial manufacture of soap remained localized, for the simple reason that since it was made of untreated animal fats, it quickly spoiled and could not be transported long distances. The development of the manufacture and mass marketing of soap in bar form is credited to Benjamin T. Babbitt, who introduced it in 1851.[23] At first, the idea seems to have met with little enthusiasm; this resistance, together with the unusually large margin of profit possible in soap manufacturing, led to some of the most intensive advertising campaigns of the nineteenth century. Overall advertising expenditures of the soap manufacturers were second only to those of patent medicine makers,[24]

and they used virtually all the available advertising media. During the 1880s, the soapmakers were particularly innovative in developing the strategy of offering free gifts, such as sets of album cards or larger prints for framing, in return for quantities of soap wrappers sent in by customers. As indicated in the detailed instructions on the backs of trade cards for David's Prize Soap, some companies also conducted contests for major prizes. However, this practice remained a much less common practice in the nineteenth century than it would become in the twentieth.

Among the roughly two hundred soap and cleanser manufacturers active in the later nineteenth century, there were several that were particularly heavy advertisers, but they varied greatly in the

77. *Lautz Brothers' Marseilles White Soap.* 1898. Knapp Company, lithographers. 5 x 3½. The Warshaw Collection of Business Americana, Smithsonian Institution.

78. *Stimson's Sudsena.* c. 1885. Wood engraving. 5 x 3½. The Warshaw Collection of Business Americana, Smithsonian Institution.

79. *Soapine (Kendall Manufacturing Company).* c. 1885. Lithograph. 6 x 4½. The Warshaw Collection of Business Americana, Smithsonian Institution.

extent to which they used trade cards. Ivory Soap and the British Pear's brand were undoubtedly the two biggest magazine advertisers, but neither of them appear frequently on trade cards. On the other hand, Enoch Morgan and Sons, who must have tried more zany publicity stunts than any other American advertiser, issued an enormous number of cards for their Sapolio cleanser. Until the end of the century, laundry detergents came in bar form just as cosmetic soaps did, and on trade cards it is sometimes difficult to determine just which kind of product is being advertised, especially since most companies marketed soaps and cleansers for a variety of uses. Bar soaps and detergents usually came in rather drab packaging; even though they were frequently pictured on trade

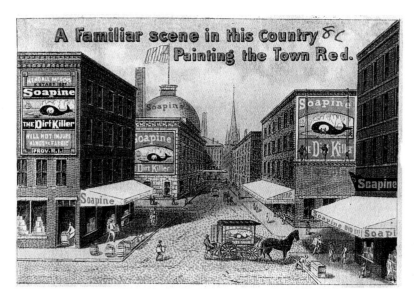

80. *Soapine (Kendall Manufacturing Company).* c. 1885. Lithograph. 3 x 4¼. Prints and Photographs Division, Library of Congress.

cards, packages were seldom as colorful as that of the Lautz Brothers' Marseilles White Soap (Fig. 77). However, for the all-purpose cleansers, which were a particularly competitive specialty within this field of manufacturing, package and trademark recognition were more heavily emphasized. In the case of Stimson's Sudsena, this extended to issuing a black-and-white trade card shaped like a box of this cleanser (Fig. 78). Like many others in this all-purpose category, the makers of Sudsena suggested that it had some special but unspecified quality that ordinary soap lacked. Perhaps the most obvious example of constantly hammering home the trademark was Soapine cleanser, made by the Kendall Company, a

firm dating from early in the century. The unmistakable trademark for Soapine was a beached whale, the side of which had been scoured to reveal a large white spot and the motto "Soapine did it." This scene appeared in a remarkable number of variations on trade cards for Kendall's product, as well as on the package itself. On one particularly exuberant card, the whale, back at sea again, carries a package of Soapine on its back (Fig. 79). Given Kendall's constant emphasis on its distinctive package in the advertising media, a card showing a town's buildings covered with it (Fig. 80) is perhaps not so far-fetched as it might seem. To a far greater extent than now, huge painted signs of this sort were a ubiquitous ele-

ment in the cityscapes of late nineteenth-century America; some can still be faintly distinguished on the sides of aged buildings.

Also prominent among the major categories of trade card advertisers were the manufacturers of food products. Like the dietary habits they reflect, patterns of advertising in this area were much different in the later nineteenth century than they are today. Many commercial food products taken for granted now were virtually nonexistent until after the turn of the century. For example, canned food production increased very slowly from 1870 to 1900 and did not see a substantial jump until after 1920.[25] Families continued to do most of their own canning and preserving in the late nineteenth century; commercially processed fruits and vegetables were rare, and canned meats were not that much more common. This was partly due to the nature of the canning industry itself, which generally did not develop totally automated processing until after 1900. Many consumers were at first suspicious of canned products, and regardless of their convenience, such products remained out of the price range of most families in any case. There were of course various bottled sauces, pickles, and other delicacies that were widely popular throughout this period, but trade cards representing even these brands are relatively rare. The rather curious specimen for Gordon and Dilworth (Fig. 81) probably had such scrupulous illustrations of the products precisely because they were so exotic to most of the buying public.

In the field of commercially prepared foods, grain-derived products showed a more rapid growth than

81. *Gordon and Dilworth Food Products.* c. 1890. J. Ottmann, lithographers. 5¼ x 3¼. The Warshaw Collection of Business Americana, Smithsonian Institution.

82. *Quaker Brand Rolled Oats.* 1895. Forbes Company, lithographers. 5 x 3. The New-York Historical Society.

market until the end of the 1870s, and most of the brands that are well known today did not exist until the late 1890s at the earliest, which was after the heyday of the illustrated trade card. For the earliest brands of breakfast food, product recognition was an especially important factor in generating sales, and trade cards for these products almost always emphasized the package. Quaker Oats, which the American Cereal Company introduced as the first mass-marketed breakfast food in 1878, provides a striking example of this tendency in a fascinating puzzle card issued in 1895 (Fig. 82). This example is typical of the marked tendency toward irregular and novelty shapes in trade cards in the last years of the century.

Other cereal products were marketed specifically as medicinal foods for infants and convalescents. Many of these were advertised very heavily in magazines and newspapers. Mellin's Food, a British import, paid fourteen thousand dollars for a colored back cover on a leading American magazine in 1893, a figure that stood for ten years as a record expenditure for a single advertisement.[26] As with patent medicines, there were usually broad claims for the restorative powers of such foods, with no indication of their contents. Trade cards for these products usually featured images of infants and children and were often aimed directly at children as consumers (Fig. 83), as much breakfast-food advertising and packaging still is.

The food products most commonly found in trade card advertising are those related to baking. Like sewing, home baking was a much more important aspect of domestic labor in the nineteenth century than it is

most others in the later nineteenth century, although consumption was still small compared to the twentieth century. Breakfast foods did not appear on the

IMPERIAL GRANUM

GREAT MEDICINAL FOOD.

A RELIABLE REMEDIAL AGENT IN ALL DISEASES OF THE STOMACH AND INTESTINES.

83. *Imperial Granum (John Carle and Sons).* c. 1890. Major and Knapp, lithographers. 3⅞ x 5¾. The Warshaw Collection of Business Americana, Smithsonian Institution.

84. *William A. Coombs Milling Company.* c. 1890. Richmond Lithographic Company, lithographers. 6⅜ x 4½. The Warshaw Collection of Business Americana, Smithsonian Institution.

today. With baking, however, the incentive was not primarily economic. Commercial bakeries existed in most towns of any size, but among prosperous families, and especially in those with servants, the commercial product was considered inferior and resorted to only when the home-baked bread ran short. Baker's bread was simply regarded as lower class.[27] For rural families, there was of course no alternative to baking at home. In either case, and regardless of whether there was any additional help in the household, baking was an important measure of the homemaker's competence. As late as 1900, scarcely 25 percent of the bread consumed in the United States was commercially baked.[28] Thus it is not surprising

that manufacturers of yeast, baking powder, and flour persistently and heavily advertised their products, especially in the years before several of the flour and baking powder companies began to merge into larger, almost monopolistic conglomerates around the turn of the century. In the 1880s and 1890s, an extraordinary variety of baking-related products was featured on trade cards; this profusion was all the greater since several of the larger milling companies produced a number of different grain-derived products, and since in the case of flour alone a single miller might advertise a number of different brand names. One Michigan milling company advertised six of its "leading brands" on a single trade card (Fig. 84).

Baking sodas and powders were fiercely competitive products in the later nineteenth century, and just as in the case of cleansers, recognition of packaging and trademarks was particularly important. The

85. *Warner's Safe Yeast.* c. 1885. Mensing and Stecher, lithographers. 5³/₈ x 4. The Warshaw Collection of Business Americana, Smithsonian Institution.

86. *Evening Star Stoves.* c. 1885. Donaldson Brothers, lithographers. 3¹/₂ x 5¹/₄. The New-York Historical Society.

trade card was a favorite medium for advertising these products, although not all of them used it to the same extent. It has been estimated that by 1893, Royal Baking Powder was the biggest newspaper advertiser in the world, using fourteen thousand newspapers in America and abroad at an annual cost of six hundred thousand dollars.[29] Yet Royal was not one of the companies that issued a large number of trade cards. Among baking products that did, few survived as brand names into the twentieth century. One conspicuous survivor is Arm and Hammer Baking Soda, which was originally just one of several brand names of soda manufactured by Church and Company. Over the years, it was found that customers actually tended to pick the Arm and Hammer brand over others marketed by the company, and as a result the other labels were dropped.[30] The Arm and Hammer package, as it appeared on late nineteenth-century trade cards, was almost exactly the same as it is today. However, among baking-related products, the prize for distinctive packaging would almost surely go to Warner's Safe Yeast. Like Soapine cleanser, it issued a great variety of trade cards that always featured the package in an emphatic manner (Fig. 85). A further indication of the emphasis this company put on its packaging can be found in the warning to the consumer on the bottom of the can not to accept any imitation that "may have been put in an old box."

One other product very prominent in trade card advertising that might be grouped with manufactured foods is coffee. Coffee companies frequently included trade cards in packages of their products, and they were particularly known for issuing large numbered series of cards that were highly fancied by

READ THIS CARD
And take this to your Grocer, and he will give you a SAMPLE FREE of

NO LABOR

ELECTRIC PASTE
SOLIDIFIED
STOVE POLISH
READY FOR USE

NO DUST

TRADE MARK REGISTERED

YOU WILL GET A PRIZE
OVER

87. *Electric Paste Stove Polish.* c. 1890. Colored wood engraving with metal type. 3 x 5 1/2. Author's collection.

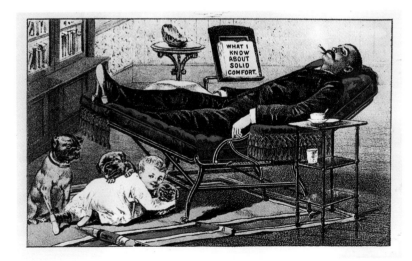

WHAT I KNOW ABOUT SOLID COMFORT.

88. *Marks Adjustable Chair Company.* c. 1885. Lithograph. 3 1/4 x 5 1/4. The Warshaw Collection of Business Americana, Smithsonian Institution.

collecting customers (on these series, see p. 93). Even though the coffee companies were extremely competitive, trademarks do not seem to have been as much of a factor with them as with many other household staples. Unlike products such as baking soda or flour, coffee packages were almost never represented on trade cards. Indeed, cards for coffee companies were unique among food products in almost never referring to the product in their illustrations, even though messages on the backs of the cards would often proclaim the superiority of the brand.

Like sewing machines, heating and cooking stoves were produced by a huge number of independent manufacturers,[31] and they are commonly encountered on trade cards. Heating stoves in particular were subject to fanciful and rapidly changing fashions of decoration, as is usually apparent on the trade cards that depict them (Fig. 86). Since stoves constantly needed to be cleaned and blacked, stove cleaning or blacking products were also commonly advertised. One somewhat crudely printed but straightforward example printed for Electric Paste stove polish is interesting in that it also serves as a coupon that could be presented to the local retailer for a free sample (Fig. 87).

Generally, other household furniture was not heavily advertised, primarily because most of it was manufactured on a local basis by small companies and, except for customers in very remote areas, was seldom transported long distances. Thus those few trade cards referring to household furniture are usually advertisements for retailers in the larger cities. Still, some of these cards provide an interesting

89. *Estey Organ Company.* c. 1885. Mayer, Merkel and Ottmann, lithographers. 3 x 5¼. Rare Books and Manuscripts Division, The New York Public Library. Astor, Lenox and Tilden Foundations.

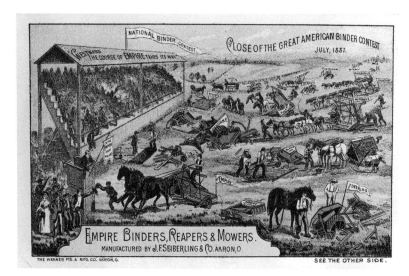

90. *Empire Binders (J. F Seiberling and Co.).* 1887. Werner Company, lithographers. 3½ x 5½. The Warshaw Collection of Business Americana, Smithsonian Institution.

record of the flamboyant and overladen decoration so common in the furniture of the later nineteenth century. There are cases of patented furniture designs that were marketed on a national scale, such as the chair in which one family man relaxes on a trade card for the Marks Adjustable Folding Chair Company (Fig. 88), but examples such as this are relatively rare in trade card advertising. One type of furniture, if it may be so classified, that was heavily advertised on trade cards was the family organ and piano. The Estey Piano and Organ Company, which had been a dominant name in this field since its foundation in the 1840s, was an especially heavy advertiser. In the later nineteenth century, the piano or organ was often the centerpiece of that almost sacrosanct room of the middle-class home, the family parlor. Enormous expenditure for the lavish furnishing of the parlor was often at the expense of the rest of the household, sometimes reaching three times the cost of any other single room. Reformist writers on domestic economy frequently condemned this preoccupation with the parlor as philistine ostentation, but seem to have gone largely unheeded.[32] In the imagery employed on most of its trade cards, the Estey company stressed the central role of its instruments in the elegantly appointed parlor and, by extension, the predominantly feminine ambiance of musicmaking in this special room of the house (Fig. 89).

In the area of durable goods, one category is especially significant in reflecting how trade cards were used to appeal to rural consumers. Perhaps more than any other product derived from heavy industry, agricultural machinery emerged in the nineteenth

91. *Ausable Horse Nail Company.* c. 1880. Hopcraft and Company, lithographers. 4¼ x 3. The Warshaw Collection of Business Americana, Smithsonian Institution.

century as a predominantly American specialty. Unlike European agriculture, which was labor intensive and characterized by relatively small farms,

American agriculture of the Great Plains typically exploited vast acreages with a small labor force. The key to this method of farming was mechanization, and in the period after the Civil War, the number of American patents granted for various implements and machines associated with agriculture was enormous. The greatest advances were made in machinery related to the harvesting of cereals, specifically the reaper and thresher. The perfection of the twine-binding harvester in 1878 and of the combined harvester and thresher around 1885 vastly increased annual grain yields. Production of wheat alone quadrupled between 1860 and 1900. Since grain was such an important element in American exports, these inventions ultimately had a considerable influence on international trade in general. By the end of the century, more than twelve thousand American patents existed for harvesting machinery alone, and more money was being invested in harvesters than any other machine in the world except for the steam engine.[33] American farm machinery had virtually no foreign competition, and was in fact a major export industry. In both the American and the foreign market, implement manufacturers were exceptionally competitive in the eighties and nineties, although they became less so as larger companies increasingly bought out smaller ones around the turn of the century. With most categories of manufactured goods, advertisers might put forward all kinds of extravagant claims about their own products but almost never mentioned their competitors by name. To this general rule, farm implement manufacturers were a notable exception. Companies frequently competed

in field trials at regional fairs and national expositions. As can be seen on a number of trade cards, makers of agricultural machinery also did not hesitate to imply that their implements would still run after their many specifically named competitors had broken down (Fig. 90). Throughout the later nineteenth century, virtually all agricultural machinery continued to be propelled by horses or other draft animals. The number of horses utilized on American farms did not in fact begin to decrease until as late as the 1920s.[34] Thus we find that particularly in the midwestern and north central states, along with numerous trade cards advertising farm implements, there were also many for hardware and veterinary products relating to farm animals. Even so pedestrian a product as horseshoe nails could become the subject of a colorful and intricately detailed trade card (Fig. 91).

In both perishable and durable goods, the list of manufactured products that were at one time or another advertised by means of the trade card could go on almost endlessly. For many of the leading advertisers, the trade card was simply one among many methods used to publicize the product. In some cases, however, the items featured on trade cards seldom if ever appear in any other advertising medium. An advertisement of the sort featured on a card for Bradley's Sea Fowl Guano (Fig. 92) would undoubtedly have seemed as inappropriate in a major family magazine of the nineteenth century as it would today. The heyday of the trade card was so relatively short that certain products that would later dominate periodical advertising appeared too late in the century to

92. *Bradley's Sea Fowl Guano.* c. 1885. Lithograph. 2⁷/₈ x 4³/₈. The Warshaw Collection of Business Americana, Smithsonian Institution.

play a major role in trade cards. For example, while there are a few unusual and highly attractive examples advertising bicycles in the late 1890s (Fig. 93), they are relatively rare as a trade card category, even though in the case of one family magazine thirty-eight different bicycle manufacturers advertised in a single issue in 1896.[35] Such exceptions taken into account, the fact remains that trade cards reveal a more diverse range of products, and tell us more about those products, than any other advertising medium used in the nineteenth century.

93. *Spalding Bicycle Company.* 1896. Lithograph. 5 x 3¹/₂. The Warshaw Collection of Business Americana, Smithsonian Institution.

CHAPTER FOUR

THE MAJOR THEMES

If only for the information they yield about nineteenth-century industry and business practices, trade cards would seem to deserve greater attention from historians than they have generally received. Yet in terms of social and cultural history, they are also significant on a broader and more fundamental level. It already has been noted that advertisers using trade cards were able to avoid the editorial constraints imposed by periodicals and other more public forms of advertising; this fact alone does much to account for the narrative richness of trade card imagery. Beyond this, however, it can easily be argued that, taken as a whole, advertising of the later nineteenth century covered an even wider range of subject matter than it has in the twentieth century. Perhaps more than any other medium, trade cards demonstrate how, in an age when photography did not yet play any appreciable role in the field, advertising was free to range from the most straightforward hard sells to the utterly fantastic. Nothing could be more brutally direct than the startling image of a fist holding a bloody club on the trade card of a Boston hat store (Fig. 94). On the other hand, a card for the Arlington collar and cuff company (Fig. 95) is charming not only for its soft and delicate colors, but also for the playful fantasy of its imagery.

Certain thematic approaches that have become commonplace in twentieth-century advertising had not yet developed to any considerable extent during the nineteenth, sexually oriented imagery being perhaps the most obvious case in point.[1] Another strategy common today, the use of the well-known celebrity, had only begun to develop. This is undoubtedly because, aside from certain political figures, there were very few personalities who would have been universally recognized in nineteenth-century America. An early example of the celebrity device was Oscar Wilde, whose appearance on many trade cards in the 1880s was prompted by his controversial lecture tour of the United States in 1882. The general reaction to Wilde's aesthetic philosophy in America is reflected in the consistent portrayal of him as the flowery, effeminate *poseur*, a caricature over which Wilde himself obviously had no more control that he had over his appearance on trade cards in the first place (Fig. 96). The major social themes of late nineteenth-century American advertising, and of trade cards in particular, reveal a society that had a firm faith in its own institutions, combined with a confident and optimistic view of its role in the progress of civilization. At the same time, that society seems in some respects to have lived in blissful and

self-imposed ignorance of the European traditions on which it was based. Given the remarkable geographic and economic expansion of the United States during the nineteenth century, this combination of self-righteous confidence and isolationism is not difficult to explain. It remains to examine the ways in which trade card advertising not only reflected, but also in many ways promoted both the positive values and the unfortunate prejudices of this dynamic and volatile society. In this context, five major thematic categories will be considered: patriotic imagery, the contrast between city and country, racial stereotypes, womanhood and the home, and finally, because of their sheer preponderance in trade card illustration, children.

It is perhaps appropriate to begin with the thematic category that was the earliest to emerge in American advertising: patriotic sentiment. Needless to say, patriotic symbols would not have the same significance in the consolidated democracy of the later nineteenth century that they had represented in the period of the Revolution, the War of 1812, or the Civil War, nor did the symbols themselves remain the same. The strident eagle and demure, classically garbed female personification of liberty that were so prevalent in the early Republic were gradually replaced by more lively

We have just convinced a party that they had better buy their Hats at Taylors,
COR. HANOVER & COURT STS. BOSTON.

94. *Taylor & Co., Hatters, Boston.* c. 1885. Mayer, Merkel and Ottmann, lithographers. 3¼ x 5½. Rare Books and Manuscripts Division, The New York Public Library. Astor, Lenox and Tilden Foundations.

95. *Arlington Collars and Cuffs.* 1888. Donaldson Brothers, lithographers. 4¾ x 3. The Warshaw Collection of Business Americana, Smithsonian Institution.

and truly popular symbols. The two primary patriotic personifications in the second half of the century were Columbia and Uncle Sam. Of the two, Uncle Sam is more readily recognized today, but Columbia was undoubtedly more important in nineteenth-century advertising. The attributes by which Columbia was known in the later nineteenth century emerged only gradually and often overlapped with earlier feminine symbols.[2] Generally, however, Columbia was specifically intended as a personification of the United States, as opposed to more broadly allegorical symbols such as Liberty or Justice. As such, she was represented as a dynamic and bounteous figure, often pictured with helmet, spear, and especially the shield with stars and stripes. Sometimes draped in the American flag, she was also occasionally represented in classical dress similar to that of ear-lier female symbols. Patriotic symbols figured prominently as trademarks from the time that the first trademark law was instituted in 1870; in fact, the first trademark granted represented an American eagle. Columbia was not long in following, as we see on an early colored trade card for America Baking Powder (Fig. 97). By the end of the century, the previously chaste and hierarchic image of Columbia had softened into a more comely and inviting figure. Martial trappings such as the spear and helmet began to disappear, to be replaced by a simple crown of stars or wreath. On a handsomely colored card for Libby's potted meats (Fig. 98), Columbia triumphantly hoists a can of the award-winning product over her head as the stars of the flag fall invitingly from her shoulder.

The figure of Uncle Sam emerged somewhat later than Columbia and, like her, went through a distinct evolution. He was preceded by a lesser-known pro-totype, Brother Jonathan. Brother Jonathan appar-

96. *Marie Fontaine's Moth & Freckle Cure.* c. 1882.
Cosack & Co., lithographers. 5¹/₄ x 3. Author's
collection.

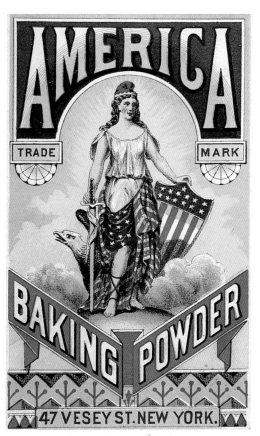

97. *America Baking Powder.* c. 1880. Lithograph.
4¹/₂ x 2³/₄. The Warshaw Collection of Business
Americana, Smithsonian Institution.

98. *Libby, McNeill and Libby Meat Products.* c. 1880.
Shober and Carqueville, lithographers. 4⁷/₈ x 2³/₄.
The Warshaw Collection of Business Americana,
Smithsonian Institution.

99. *Mrs. Potts' Cold Handle Sad Irons.* c. 1880. Lithograph. 3 x 4¹/₄. Author's collection.

the frequent presence of either Uncle Sam or Columbia had a deeper symbolic significance. Along with grain crops, meat products played an extremely important role in American exports throughout the nineteenth century. In the seventies and eighties, however, American meat products met not only with increased competition but also with considerable resistance in the protectionist markets of Europe. Much to the dismay of the Chicago meat packers, American pork was for a time boycotted by several European countries to protect their own producers. American exporters responded by pushing their products all the more energetically. Earlier in the century, meat had been shipped in large wooden barrels; in the 1870s, Americans introduced two important innovations, refrigerated shipping and canned meat products. In the area of processed foods, canned meats would become the most significant product both at home and abroad. The two giants of the industry, Libby McNeill and J. A. Wilson, both claimed patents on the characteristic tapered corned beef can.[4] In the 1880s, both companies also stressed their canned beef as a sort of universal convenience food and featured the can on a great variety of trade cards. The Libby McNeill card showing Uncle Sam offering a can of corned beef to England's John Bull mirrors the fact that England was indeed the greatest consumer of processed meats from America (Fig. 100). On cards for J. A. Wilson, their product is enjoyed equally by Prussian officers and French gourmands.

ently first appeared during the American Revolution and may have been a symbolic representation of Jonathan Trumbull the elder, then governor of Connecticut. Brother Jonathan was an impudent, shrewd Yankee, lanky in build and, until the eve of the Civil War, clean-shaven. Meanwhile, the figure of Uncle Sam, based on a real person who gained a certain notoriety as an army supplier during the War of 1812, quickly gained currency around midcentury and by the 1870s had largely supplanted Brother Jonathan as a male patriotic symbol.[3] Nevertheless, in a trade card for Mrs. Potts' Irons, which probably dates from the early 1880s (Fig. 99), the figure in the kitchen with Miss Columbia is named Brother Jonathan and

intones a New England accent even though he clearly has the physical attributes of Uncle Sam. Although his costume was predictable enough, Uncle Sam's apparent age and physical features varied considerably in later nineteenth-century representations. As a character in trade card imagery, Uncle Sam was represented as a sort of spokesman and salesman for American enterprise; he is repeatedly shown presenting a product for the amazed admiration of the rest of the world. In most cases, this was largely a rhetorical gesture, since most of the products represented on trade cards were intended primarily for the domestic rather than the foreign market.

In the case of advertisements for processed meats,

Another highly visible patriotic symbol that caught the imagination of Americans in the 1880s had

100. *Libby, McNeill and Libby Meat Products.* c. 1880. Shober and Carqueville, lithographers. 2³/₄ x 4⁷/₈. The Warshaw Collection of Business Americana, Smithsonian Institution.

come to them as a gift from France. The Statue of Liberty had already created an enormous sensation even before it was officially dedicated by President Cleveland in October 1886. When this monument was completed, trade cards were at the height of their popularity. Not surprisingly, the Statue of Liberty soon appeared on trade cards advertising all kinds of products, especially since such a large number of commercial lithographers who printed trade cards were themselves located in New York City. On one card, the French Marianne bestows a gift of Parisian Sauce on Columbia, as if in solidarity with the American Republic; in the background, the Statue of Liberty dominates the harbor (Fig. 101). (This exotic condiment was actually manufactured by d'Oliveira

and Company of New York.) Some representations of the monument appeared on trade cards even before it was finished, often with details that differ considerably from the finished monument. The statue itself was used to endorse a great number of different products, and in a fairly predictable manner. Liberty is usually shown either standing upon or holding up a package of the product, and sometimes she can be seen doing both (Fig. 102).

Although overt political references are seldom seen in trade cards, they occasionally reflect the excitement generated over presidential elections, especially in the 1880s and 1890s, when these contests were very close. In some cases, it would appear that the advertisers responsible for the card clearly favored one

101. *Parisian Sauce (d'Oliveira and Co., New York).* c. 1887. Mayer, Merkel and Ottmann, lithographers. 5¹/₈ x 3¹/₈. The New-York Historical Society.

102. *Brainerd and Armstrong Thread.* c. 1887. Mayer, Merkel and Ottmann, lithographers. 5¼ x 3. Rare Books and Manuscripts Division, The New York Public Library. Astor, Lenox and Tilden Foundations.

103. *Muzzy's Sun Gloss Starch.* 1884. Lithograph. 3⅜ x 6. The Warshaw Collection of Business Americana, Smithsonian Institution.

political party over the other. In 1884, a trade card for Muzzy's Starch congratulated the Republican ticket of Blaine and Logan (Fig. 103). The winner of that election, Grover Cleveland, entered the White House a bachelor. Two years later, he created news that was enthusiastically received throughout the nation when he married Francis Folsom, an attractive and popular Washington socialite who was his former ward and twenty-eight years his junior. A card for Merrick's Thread was just one of several that immediately exploited this sensational marriage in a most sentimental manner (Fig. 104). On the occasion of the fiercely contested election of 1900, one company issued a card on which Columbia holds out the President Suspender to the two candidates, William McKinley and William Jennings Bryan (Fig. 105). On the back of the card, suspender customers were invited to enter a contest to guess the popular vote of the election.

The last year in the nineteenth century in which the United States had an unfavorable balance of trade was 1892. In addition to the traditional mainstays of agricultural products and raw materials, America was now exporting machinery and other industrially produced goods on an unprecedented scale. Perhaps even more significant was the sudden emergence of America as a major military power. In the last ten years of the nineteenth century, the United States attained a degree of military might relative to other industrialized nations that it had never enjoyed before. Fired by jingoistic newspapers, Americans enthusiastically supported the declaration of war on Spain in 1898; two years later, the United States was an imperialist power in good standing, having acquired

Cuba, Puerto Rico, Hawaii, and the Philippines. Given the prosperity, optimism, and confident nationalism of Americans in the 1890s, it might at first seem surprising that trade cards of this decade did not have a more patriotic flavor. It must be remembered, however, that by the nineties, the card-collecting phenomenon had begun to fade in popularity, and the larger advertising budgets had started to shift into other advertising media. One of the most common patriotic references in trade cards around the end of the century was to the Great White Fleet. In this regard, a stock card with the grandiose image of the Battleship Maine (Fig. 106) seems ironic, given that ship's fate in Havana harbor in 1898.

While references to the specific political attitudes of late nineteenth-century Americans were not particularly common in trade card advertising, allusions to their social and racial views certainly were, and to a greater extent here than in any other advertising medium. Racial prejudices of the later nineteenth century have been treated in a variety of historical literature, but surprisingly little attention has been given to their pervasiveness in advertising. By present standards, the racial caricatures seen in late nineteenth-century advertising seem shockingly direct and unabashed. In such racially oriented imagery, references to blacks are by far the most frequently encountered, and for obvious reasons. White attitudes toward blacks began to change rapidly after the Civil War, especially when the full impact of emancipation began to be felt in the North. At first, this impact was primarily economic; the wholesale influx of blacks into the northern states, culminating

104. *Merrick Thread.* 1886. Donaldson Brothers, lithographers. 4½ x 3. The Warshaw Collection of Business Americana, Smithsonian Institution.

in the so-called Exodus of 1879, created new economic pressures and intense friction in industrial cities. By the beginning of the 1880s, fears and prejudice on the part of northern whites took on specifically

105. *The President Suspender Company.* 1900. American Lithography Company, lithographers. 5½ x 3⅜. The Warshaw Collection of Business Americana, Smithsonian Institution.

106. *Joseph J. Mandery, Bicycle Dealer, Rochester, N. Y.* c. 1895. Lithograph. 4 x 6¹/₈. The Warshaw Collection of Business Americana, Smithsonian Institution.

107. *Sanford's Ginger.* c. 1885. Forbes and Company, lithographers. 4¹/₂ x 3. Rare Books and Manuscripts Division, The New York Public Library. Astor, Lenox and Tilden Foundations.

political connotations as well. While the nation was still somewhat divided on the issue of black suffrage, several prominent editors and columnists in the North began to advocate reconciliation with the South on the basis of antiblack sentiment. Writing for the influential *Century* magazine in 1883, Richard Watson Gilder proclaimed that ". . . the negroes constitute a peasantry wholly untrained in, and ignorant of, those ideas of constitutional liberty and progress which are the birthright of every white voter . . . they are gregarious and emotional rather than intelligent, and are easily led in any direction by white men of energy and determination."[5] Thus in addition to the economic threat they seemed to pose in the North, blacks were also increasingly looked upon as a source of rampant political corruption. Further evidence of the changing racial mood of the nation came when the Civil Rights Act of 1875 was declared unconstitutional in 1883, opening the way for widespread discrimination against blacks in public places. Regardless of their true economic and political impact, blacks were viewed as a threat by northern city dwellers as never before, and since most publishers and advertisers were located in the northern cities, it is not surprising that throughout the 1880s blacks were treated with varying degrees of derision in the advertising media.

Taken as a whole, the image of blacks in trade cards is somewhat ambiguous. We have seen how on a trade card printed by J. H. Bufford just before the

108. *St. Louis Beef Canning Company.* c. 1885.
Wemple and Company, lithographers. 4³/₄ x 3.
The Warshaw Collection of Business Americana,
Smithsonian Institution.

109. *Nigger Head Tobacco (William S. Kimball and
Co.).* c. 1885. Clay and Company, lithographers.
4¹/₂ x 3. The Warshaw Collection of Business
Americana, Smithsonian Institution.

110. *Max Stadler and Company Clothiers, New York.*
c. 1885. Bufford Company, lithographers. 5 x 3¹/₄.
The Warshaw Collection of Business Americana,
Smithsonian Institution.

Civil War (Fig. 35), the black maid, however rude her physical features, is still treated more or less sympathetically. This paternalistic but essentially positive image of the faithful black servant lingered for some time in the work of sentimental artists and novelists.[6] In the more straightforward and ruthlessly pervasive media of advertising, such generosity disappeared rapidly. The black was usually represented as a simple and good-natured soul, always lazy, often ridiculous, but never malicious or dangerous. The poor rural black of the South was the predominant stereotype, as in the case of the girl with an infant in a watermelon cradle (Fig. 107). The needs of this stereotypical black were few, and, as suggested in a none-too-subtle fashion on the card of a St. Louis packing company (Fig. 108), usually revolved around food. Alternatively, there was also the urbanized black dandy living beyond his economic station, as indicated by the gaudy and pretentious clothing he invariably wore. A typical example is the namesake of Nigger Head Tobacco (Fig. 109). (Perhaps because of its associations with the South, tobacco advertising featured blacks more consistently than any other kind of product.) An even more grotesque caricature of this sort can be seen on the trade card of a retail clothier of New York (Fig. 110). A great many late nineteenth-century trade cards were intended to be comical, and just as in minstrel shows and other forms of popular entertainment, the black was an ever-popular comic vehicle. This, perhaps more than any other single factor, accounts for the pervasiveness of blacks as subjects on trade cards. Certain comic themes were used over and over again, regardless of

the product advertised. For years, the Lautz Brothers company circulated a picture of a black lad being scrubbed white by their soap, with the slogan "beat that if you can" (Fig. 111). It was only one of several soaps, cleansers, and stove polishes that were shown to accomplish the same thing.

However fantastic some interpretations might have been, the American Indian had served as a symbol of America in European art and literature almost from the time that the new continent was discovered. In the eighteenth century, the Indian princess became an important allegorical figure in the American colonies, symbolizing not only their trade and commerce but also, with the arrival of the Revolution, their striving for liberty.[7] As shown on several trade cards engraved by Abel Bowen (Fig. 14, for example), the Indian had remained a symbol of the bounteous natural resources of America in the early nineteenth century as well. During the heyday of trade cards in the 1880s, the American Indian was almost as common a source of imagery as were blacks.[8] Yet ironically, while Indians were usually depicted with greater dignity in advertising, the treatment they actually received from the government and other institutions was even worse than that to which blacks were subjected. The inexorable expansion that had begun pushing Indian tribes further west earlier in the century gathered momentum after the Civil War, largely because the Indian was at odds with the overwhelming interests of the railroads. After the railroads came the great surge of settlers. The Indian territories between Kansas and Texas had a population of 7,000 in 1880; by 1889, five years after the railroad had come

111. *Lautz Brothers and Company Soaps.* c. 1880. Colored Engraving. $4^1/_2$ x 3. Rare Books and Manuscripts Division, The New York Public Library. Astor, Lenox and Tilden Foundations.

through this area, that population had increased to 110,000.[9] By the end of the 1880s, the Indian was little more than a romanticized abstraction for most white Americans, and was seen firsthand only in

112. *Indian Queen Perfume (Bean and Brother Co.).* c. 1885. Lithograph. 4 x 2⅝. Rare Books and Manuscripts Division, The New York Public Library. Astor, Lenox and Tilden Foundations.

113. *Davis' Indian Herb Remedy.* c. 1885. Karle and Company, lithographers. 3 x 4¾. The Warshaw Collection of Business Americana, Smithsonian Institution.

medicine and wild west shows, if at all. Having only briefly interfered in the great western expansion of the nation, the Indian had duly disappeared, and in doing so had once again become exotic. This exotic appeal in turn made the Indian a natural vehicle for advertising.

As a subject that was intrinsically American and exotic at the same time, the Indian figured in the advertising of all kinds of products, often in a most incongruous manner. The image of the demure and elegantly attired young thing extracting the essence from a flower for Indian Queen Perfume (Fig. 112) is surely as far removed from reality as any of the noble savages of the eighteenth-century Enlightenment. In the case of patent medicines, however, associations

with popular mythology surrounding the Indian were much more specific. The myriad Indian potions and remedies sold in the nineteenth century were marketed on the assumption that the red man, in his unique communion with nature, possessed knowledge of its curative powers unrevealed to civilized man. Unrevealed, that is, until the medicine company in question had by some fortunate circumstance gained that knowledge from the Indian.[10] On a rather clumsily rendered trade card for Davis' Indian Herb Remedy (Fig. 113), the Indian is typically surrounded by the majesty of nature, the only sign of civilization being the bottle he pensively holds in front of him. On the other hand, a card for the Ayer Company would seem to indicate that the Indian

114. *Ayers Pills.* c. 1885.
Lithograph. 3¹/₄ x 5. The
Warshaw Collection of
Business Americana,
Smithsonian Institution.

115. *Libby, McNeill and
Libby Meat Products.*
c. 1880. Shober and
Carqueville, lithographers.
2³/₄ x 4⁷/₈. The Warshaw
Collection of Business
Americana, Smithsonian
Institution.

could benefit from white man's medicine as well, as a distinctly out-of-sorts brave is offered one of Ayer's pills by his dutiful squaw (Fig. 114). In numerous instances Indians are represented as being quite delighted to suddenly encounter certain of the white man's manufactured products, as in the scene where, having massacred the members of a wagon train, the raiding party gleefully helps itself to cans of Libby McNeill corned beef (Fig. 115). Like so many dime novels of the period, this card presents a view of the Indian that was acceptable in advertising precisely because it no longer had any basis in reality.

However rude certain caricatures of the black and the Indian may have been, both were represented as essentially benign and unthreatening. In the case of another racial minority, however, trade card advertising perpetuated an even narrower and more malicious stereotype. Images of the Chinese do not occur as frequently on trade cards, but where they do, they are almost invariably treated in a most insulting manner. Again, it is important to consider the rapidly changing racial demography of late nineteenth-century America to account for this. In response to the need for cheap manual labor in the Far West, Chinese immigration to the United States increased at an extraordinary rate between 1850 and 1880. Already by 1870, the Chinese comprised fully 25 percent of the working population of California. In response to what was widely perceived as the economic and cultural threat of this alien population, vicious riots against the Chinese broke out in a number of Pacific Coast cities during the 1870s. In California, a white Workingmen's party was formed with the expressed

116. *Mrs. Potts' Cold Handle Sad Irons.* c. 1880. W. Boell and Company, lithographers. 2¾ x 4½. The Warshaw Collection of Business Americana, Smithsonian Institution.

purpose of getting rid of cheap Chinese labor "as soon as possible."[11] Resistance to Chinese immigration was by no means limited to the Pacific Coast. Anxious to tap this cheap and efficient source of labor, industrialists in the northeast began bringing Chinese into their factories in the 1870s, often using them as strike breakers, which brought on a hysterical reaction from white workers.[12] Anticipating restrictions on further immigration, eighteen thousand Chinese entered the United States in 1880–1881, and over thirty-nine thousand arrived in 1882. At this point, the United States Congress stepped in. The Chinese Exclusion Act of 1882 not only barred additional Chinese from entering the country, but also declared those already here ineligible for American citizenship. The bill received wide geographical support, reflecting the belief that the Chinese posed an economic threat in many parts of the country.

Whatever the economic factors, there was also a more deep-seated cultural and racial bias against the Chinese. Shortly after the Civil War, the *New York Times,* after complaining about the four million "degraded" blacks in the South, went on to exclaim that ". . . if there were to be a flood-tide of Chinese population—a population befouled with all the social vices, with no knowledge or appreciation of free institutions or constitutional liberty, with heathenish souls and heathenish propensities, whose character, and habits, and modes of thought are firmly fixed by the consolidating influences of ages upon ages—we

117. *Celluloid Collars.* c. 1880. Lithograph. 5½ x 3¼. The Warshaw Collection of Business Americana, Smithsonian Institution.

should be prepared to bid farewell to republicanism . . . ."[13] Although they may have had their own strong work ethic, the Chinese "heathen" were held to possess none of the moral or religious values shared by Christian America. Clever and industrious, they could neither be kept in economic servitude like the black nor simply forgotten like the Indian. In short, they were considered to be impossible to assimilate into American society. The flow of Chinese immigration may have stopped in 1882, but if the messages of numerous trade cards are any indication, sentiment to rid the country of those Chinese that had already arrived was strong. These images give the impression that all the Chinese in America were engaged in laundry work. Like a Pied Piper, the Uncle Sam on one card lures hordes of Chinese from California back to China with a supply of flat irons (Fig. 116). On another card, Columbia literally indicates the handwriting on the wall: with the advent of Celluloid collars and cuffs, cheap Chinese labor could be shown the door (Fig. 117).

Interestingly, the characterization of the Japanese, who had not immigrated into the United States in such considerable numbers, was utterly different from that of the Chinese. American fascination with Japan began when Perry opened the country to the West in the 1850s and was reinforced by the influence that European *Japonisme* had on certain aesthetically cultivated Americans later in the century. However, much of the impetus for the popularity of things Japanese in the 1880s was the extraordinary success of Gilbert and Sullivan's *Mikado* in the American theater. Opening at New York's Fifth Avenue Theatre in

118. *White Borax Soap (Allen B. Wrisley Co).* c. 1886. Lithograph. 4$^{1}/_{4}$ x 3. The Warshaw Collection of Business Americana, Smithsonian Institution.

the fall of 1885, the *Mikado* was such a hit that, by the following year, it was being presented in a German version in another New York theater. Themes from other Gilbert and Sullivan operettas were also rela-

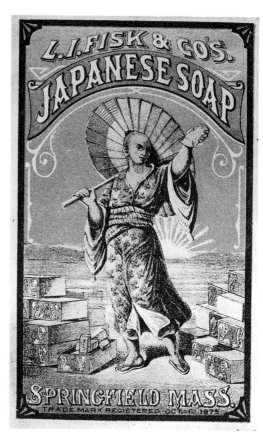

119. *Japanese Soap (L. I. Fisk and Co.).* c. 1880. Lithograph. 5$^{3}/_{4}$ x 3. Rare Books and Manuscripts Division, The New York Public Library. Astor, Lenox and Tilden Foundations.

120. *Victor Shade Rollers.* c. 1885. Calvert Lithography Company, lithographers. 3 x 5. Author's collection.

tively common in trade cards of the 1880s,[14] but *Mikado* characters such as Yum-Yum or the three little maids from school were particularly popular. Like the actors that played these parts on stage, the *Mikado* characters shown on such cards are usually Japanese in costume only (Fig. 118). Where true Japanese culture was represented, it was as the essence of oriental exoticism and refinement, and was thus a favorite vehicle for the marketing of perfumed soaps and other luxury articles (Fig. 119).

Despite the enormous influx of European immigrants in the last twenty years of the century, references to specific groups on trade cards were few. This is undoubtedly due in large part to the fact that such immigrants made up a considerable part of the consumers that advertisers were trying to attract. The Irish maid or cook, the "Bridget" just off the boat, shows up here and there, as does the occasional rotund German. These were generally good-natured parodies, usually lampooning language more than physical appearances, although in the case of the two Irish tenement housewives shown on a card for a brand of curtain rollers (Fig. 120) there is clearly a touch of both. The Jew, who was so frequently the brunt of bitter caricature in European popular illustration, was treated much better in America. There were a few satires of the Jewish traveling salesman or tailor (Fig. 121), but these were extremely rare. Since so many of the major lithographic companies were in New York and were owned and operated by Jewish immigrants from Europe, the few examples that do exist were usually printed in other

121. *Bell's Pond Lily Soap.* c. 1885. Gies and Company, lithographers. 5½ x 3. The Warshaw Collection of Business Americana, Smithsonian Institution.

cities. Italians, who formed another of the largest immigrant groups, scarcely appear at all except as highly romanticized inhabitants of the old country, such as the mother and child on a card for Jayne's Balsam (Fig. 122).

It is perhaps difficult for most Americans living in the twentieth century to comprehend fully the gulf that existed between urban and rural life in this country throughout most of the nineteenth century. From an economic standpoint, one of the greatest differences between city and country was the availability of consumer goods. Although the railroads, along with Rural Free Delivery and the phenomenon of mail-order buying it spawned, would bring about a greater uniformity of consumption in the last years of the century, many things that city residents took for granted could be had by their rural counterparts only through considerable effort or travel, if at all. Like the range of products advertised, the way in which advertising was employed naturally differed greatly between urban and small town or rural environments. While trade cards certainly reflected basic differences in consumer habits, the scale of their distribution also tended to progressively erase some of these distinctions. For trade cards advertising mass-marketed goods, the most significant factor to bear in mind is that most were printed in the larger cities, and especially in New York. This became all the more true toward the end of the century when many smaller lithographic firms began to be swallowed up by larger ones. Thus the view of both city and country expressed in trade card imagery was essentially one generated by commercial illustrators

122. *Jayne's Carminative Balsam.* c. 1885. Major and Knapp, lithographers. 3¹/₈ x 4⁵/₈. Author's collection.

and printers working in New York and a handful of other eastern cities. The overall result was that while trade cards often permit interesting and authentic glimpses of urban life, the view of country life and the West, just like the characterization of the American Indian, was usually an ill-informed and highly idyllic one.

As with earlier examples, trade cards of the later nineteenth century provide valuable insights into the architectural complexion of the larger cities. This was especially true in New York, not only because of the exceptional amount of commercial printing done there, but also because the city had entered a period of vigorous building activity, producing architectural

achievements that were unique in the nation. Beyond this, many trade cards produced in New York were specifically for local distribution, to an audience that was either familiar with the architectural monuments or, in the case of department stores and other commercial buildings, intended to become familiarized with them. In terms of both local and national distribution, no city was more commonly represented on trade cards than New York, and it ultimately served as the archetypal city upon which the impression of urban life was frequently based. Certain images of the city, such as the exuberant scene on a card for the Colgate Company's Rapid Transit Soap (Fig. 123), must have seemed marvelous indeed to res-

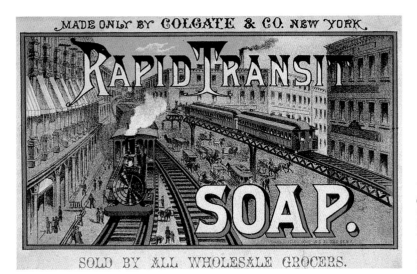

123. *Rapid Transit Soap (Colgate and Co.).* c. 1885. Charles Shields and Sons, lithographers. 3¹/₂ x 5⁵/₈. The Warshaw Collection of Business Americana, Smithsonian Institution.

124. *Willimantic Thread Co.* c. 1883. Forbes Co., lithographers. 3³/₈ x 4¹/₂. The Warshaw Collection of Business Americana, Smithsonian Institution.

idents of rural and small-town America.

We have already seen the way in which enthusiasm for the Statue of Liberty was reflected in various trade cards. Another monument built in this period that instilled great pride in the nation and in New Yorkers in particular was the Brooklyn Bridge. Begun in 1870, the bridge was perhaps the greatest engineering marvel in America when it was finished in 1883. Even if they could not do so in real life, any number of advertisers used the bridge as a monumental backdrop for advertising their products on trade cards (Fig. 124). On one especially fanciful card for a shoe manufacturer, the Brooklyn Bridge links two gigantic "cable screw wire" shoes on either side of the East River (Fig. 125). Although not specifically dated, the reference to the amount of wire used in this com-

pany's shoes in 1874 suggests that this is a relatively early color trade card, and one which in fact represents the bridge several years before its completion.

The manner in which certain architectural subjects were manifested on trade cards resulted from the desire of retailers and manufacturers to impress their customers with the scale of their facilities. Both in terms of their specialized, functional design and the scale on which they marketed manufactured goods, the department stores that developed so rapidly in the years after the Civil War have been compared with the largest factories of the period.[15] Although the idea did not originate in the United States, American department stores, building on the pioneering efforts of Alexander Stewart in New York and John Wanamaker in Philadelphia, were characterized by a size and variety of goods unparalleled elsewhere. Large urban department stores led the way in placing full-page illustrated advertisements in city newspapers. With increasing railroad links between cities and outlying areas, many leading department stores also advertised in small-town newspapers, offering special incentives, including even free transportation, to lure the country folk to do their shopping in the city.[16] Whether distributed in the cities where the stores themselves were located or in areas further afield, trade cards for department stores also served an important advertising function. In New York, where competition between department stores was naturally quite keen, a large number of stores issued cards of exceptional quality, with further information about their wares and special sales often indicated on the back. Cards that included illustrations of the

125. *Cable Screw Wire Boots and Shoes.* c. 1875. Donaldson Brothers, engravers. 3¼ x 6⅜. Rare Books and Manuscripts Division, The New York Public Library. Astor, Lenox and Tilden Foundations.

126. *Vogel Brothers, Clothiers, New York.* c. 1885. Lithograph. 3⅛ x 4⅝. The Warshaw Collection of Business Americana, Smithsonian Institution.

stores were clearly meant to impress by the sheer magnitude of the structures. The trade card for one New York clothes retailer pictured both of its imposing Manhattan outlets side by side (Fig. 126). Another clothier's card showed not only the exterior of the store but also one of its extraordinarily expansive sales floors (Fig. 127).

As seen in both of these cards, department stores and other large retail outlets frequently stressed their clearly marked, "one price" marketing policy; their high-volume sales and rapid turnover allowed such stores to dramatically reduce prices on clothing and other essential consumer items. Again, the close parallel between the factory and the department store becomes evident. The manufactured goods produced in ever-larger quantities by factory workers were made more affordable to those same workers by the mass-marketing techniques of department stores. It would be a mistake to assume that nineteenth-century advertising separated or concealed the integral links between the production of the factory and the consumption of the retail store, that it denied the labor of its audience, as so much twentieth-century advertising has done.[17] On the contrary, in a way that may seem curious to the twentieth-century observer, nineteenth-century manufacturers took great pride in demonstrating to the public the magnitude of their factories, down to the last fuming smokestack. A modern oil company would be unlikely to boast of its industrial facilities in the grandiose manner with which the Pratt Oil Company represented its Brooklyn refinery in the 1880s (Fig. 128). The frequent depiction of majestic factories on trade cards is

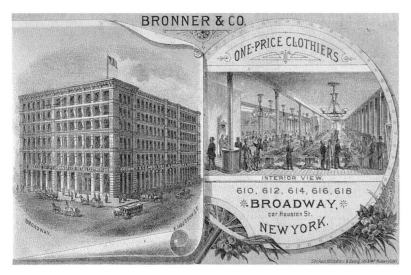

127. *Bronner and Company, Clothiers, New York.* c. 1885. Sackett, Wilhelms and Betzig, lithographers. 3¹/₂ x 5¹/₂. The Warshaw Collection of Business Americana, Smithsonian Institution.

128. *Charles Pratt and Company, Refiners.* c. 1885. Lithograph. 6 x 3⁷/₈. The New-York Historical Society.

129. *Fleischmann's Yeast.* c. 1875. Lithograph. 3¹/₄ x 5¹/₄. The Warshaw Collection of Business Americana, Smithsonian Institution.

simply further proof of the obvious confidence and optimism with which nineteenth-century Americans looked upon the industrial revolution taking place around them. A black-and-white card for the

130. *McCormick Harvester Company.* Cosack and Company, lithographers. 3¹/₂ x 6¹/₈. The Warshaw Collection of Business Americana, Smithsonian Institution.

131. *Hansen's Dairyman's Products.* c. 1885. Gies and Company, lithographers. 3¹/₂ x 5⁷/₈. Author's collection.

Fleischmann Yeast Company, dating from the 1870s, not only shows the extent of its factory site, but also goes into some detail on the capacity of what is proudly claimed as the largest yeast manufactory in the world (Fig. 129). In the 1880s and 1890s, a common practice was to depict the factory of the advertiser on the reverse side of the trade card, usually in black and white. As in the case of the Fleischmann card, these views were often accompanied by a reference to the prodigious manufacturing capacity of the factory. In short, the size of the factory and the scale of its production were presented to the public as the ultimate assurance of the quality of the product being advertised. Given the intense competition in that field of heavy industry, it is not surprising that a card for the McCormick Company (Fig. 130) should offer a bombastic view of its harvester works, claimed to be the largest in the world. To reinforce the point, a vignette within this illustration depicts the corporate headquarters of the company in Chicago. Although most of the great industries advertised in trade cards were located in the larger cities, some mills and factories were also shown to be located in a literally pastoral setting. Hansen's Dairyman's Products was a Danish company, but as indicated on the back of its bucolic trade card (Fig. 131), its American manufactory was located "on a picturesque island in the beautiful Mohawk River, at Little Falls, N.Y."

Some trade cards indicate that, much like today, urban dwellers of the later nineteenth century were eager to escape the summer heat of the city for the seashore or mountain resort. As early as 1878, one New York excursion boat company issued a card

132. *White Steamer Company, New York.* 1878. Lithograph. $3^{1}/_{4}$ x $5^{3}/_{8}$ (folded out). The Warshaw Collection of Business Americana, Smithsonian Institution.

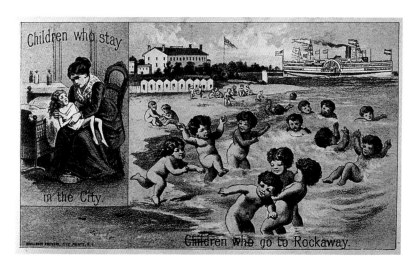

133. *White Steamer Company, New York.* c. 1880. Donaldson Brothers, lithographers. $3^{1}/_{2}$ x $5^{3}/_{8}$. Prints and Photographs Division, Library of Congress.

describing the pleasures awaiting city dwellers at Rockaway Beach (Fig. 132). In the terminology of collectors, this is a metamorphic card, a type frequently encountered among late nineteenth-century trade cards. The area showing the beach house on the right folds back to reveal ladies in bathing garments. Another card for the same steamer company is more to the point: by contrast to the health of the children shown frolicking on the beach, disease and misery await the wretched child confined in the heat of the city (Fig. 133). Given prevailing sanitary conditions, widespread fears about remaining in the city in the summer months were justifiable enough. Unrelieved urban habitation without the restorative benefits of nature was widely believed to have an adverse effect on mental as well as physical health, especially in the case of women. For those women diagnosed as suffering from "hysteria" and other mental afflictions, a lengthy rest in the country was considered to be the most efficacious cure. The cure, like the disease, was essentially confined to the prosperous middle and upper classes.[18] In certain cases, trade cards also reflect the growing trend toward suburban living in the late nineteenth century, the most striking examples being the surprisingly numerous cards advertising lawn mowers. It is interesting to note that the mowers advertised by various manufacturers almost invariably are shown being delicately pushed about by elegantly dressed women or children (Fig. 134). Such representations were undoubtedly intended to demonstrate the easy operation of these machines, but also suggested that the labor of mowing a lawn was a genteel activity of wealthy suburban dwellers.

134. *Charter Oak Mowers.* c. 1885. Schumacher and Ettlinger, lithographers. 3 x 5¹⁄₂. The Warshaw Collection of Business Americana, Smithsonian Institution.

135. *The "Old Reliable" Shuttler Wagon.* c. 1885. Clay and Richmond, lithographers. 3¹⁄₄ x 5³⁄₄. The Warshaw Collection of Business Americana, Smithsonian Institution.

Views of life in the country as expressed on trade cards were at least as common as those showing life in the city, but were seldom as authentic. The farmer and the western settler were little understood and frequently romanticized by purveyors of advertising. Such misunderstanding is only one aspect of the larger mythology surrounding agrarian life that was so resolutely promoted and maintained throughout the century. As Henry Nash Smith observed in his classic study of western expansion, the agrarian ideal as the prevailing view of the West had an extraordinary longevity in nineteenth-century America.[19] Given the enormous importance of grain exports in the overall balance of trade, Americans fully appreciated the economic significance of the territories west of the Mississippi, and a new wave of settlement in the area beginning in the 1870s seemed to promise new prosperity for the region and the nation. Much of what happened in the 1880s, however, should have soured this optimistic view. Predictions that increasing rainfall would naturally follow the cultivation of the plains did not come to pass. Periods of severe drought repeatedly drove back advancing settlement in the years between 1870 and 1890. In the early 1880s, depressed commodity prices brought extreme hardship in the West; Kansas farmers were so hard-pressed that they burned their corn for fuel rather than shipping it to market. Finally, there was the catastrophic winter of 1885–1886, so severe that it essentially halted the western immigration that had been increasing over the previous decade. Trade cards that extolled the simple but prosperous life of the western plains in the 1880s did so at a time when economic

THE TRADE CARD IN NINETEENTH-CENTURY AMERICA

Farm Job, showing water delivered in different fields, with valve tanks. Erected by B. S. Williams & Co., Kalamazoo, Mich.

136. *B. S. Williams and Company Windmills.* c. 1885. H. Gugler and Sons, lithographers. 3⅛ x 6. The Warshaw Collection of Business Americana, Smithsonian Institution.

ARRIVAL OF THE NO. 8 WHEELER & WILSON.

137. *Wheeler and Wilson Sewing Machine Company.* c. 1885. Forbes and Company, lithographers. 3 x 5. Author's collection.

and climatic conditions over much of the region were creating a profound crisis.

Regardless of geographical location, the image of rural America presented on trade cards was invariably one of great serenity and pastoral beauty. In its own way, a trade card for a farm wagon (Fig. 135) can tell as much about the continuing romantic fixation with the American landscape as a Currier and Ives print or an easel painting. Like the image of the landscape itself, the degree to which the latest agricultural technology displayed on some trade cards was actually employed is questionable. In reality, few farms had such imposing buildings and well-ordered plots as those shown in the ideal agrarian setting portrayed by one Michigan windmill manufacturer (Fig. 136). Still, the extent to which farming and the raising of livestock were possible at all in some regions depended on the introduction of the windmill in the seventies and eighties.

Trade cards for sewing machines frequently represented scenes of rural life. Considering the importance of this appliance to families living in isolated areas, the special occasion of the arrival of the new Wheeler and Wilson represented on one card (Fig. 137) was probably not much exaggerated. On the other hand, the scene showing the "New Home" in the Far West (Fig. 138), dating from 1881, undoubtedly painted a far rosier picture of the settler's homestead than actually existed over most of the plains at this time. Like the myth surrounding the American Indian, the image of a frontier utopia lingered in advertising long after events showed that image to be false.

138. *New Home Sewing Machine Company.* 1881. W. J. Morgan and Company, lithographers. 3 x 5. Author's collection.

A striking fact about the representation of the sexes in trade card imagery is that while men appear relatively seldom and in fairly predictable situations (farm machinery, men's clothing, etc.), women are encountered in a much broader range of contexts so far as the products advertised are concerned. In retrospect, the frequency with which women appear in trade card imagery, and in advertising in general, is easy enough to explain. First, one must consider that women constituted the majority of general-magazine readers in the later nineteenth century and that a large number of magazines were specifically intended for a female audience. Those same magazines were heavily laden with advertisements for women's and household products. In an article published in *Advertising Age* in 1891, Nathaniel Fowler recommended that since women made most of the purchasing decisions of the household, manufacturers would do well to direct their messages toward them.[20] There can be little question that from periodicals alone, women were exposed to a greater volume of general advertising than men. This was even more true with trade cards, which were much more likely to be acquired and saved by women than by men in the first place. Thus a high percentage of the goods heavily advertised by means of trade cards were precisely those selected by the woman of the house.

However frequently it may occur, the image of women in trade cards is generally a narrow and stereotypical one. Reflecting the overall view concerning her position in nineteenth-century society, woman was almost invariably represented as the dutiful wife and loving mother. Needless to say, women's roles have changed enormously since the nineteenth century; however, the justifications put forward for the more confined and restricted position of women in the last century are perhaps still only partially understood today. While there is certainly no lack of nineteenth-century literature addressing this issue, the attitudes expressed in that literature are complex and often ambiguous. On the one hand, women were assumed to be both mentally and physically inferior to men, their more delicate nervous constitutions rendering them ill-suited to the world of business. In the realm of politics, the involvement of women was judged as not just inappropriate but dangerous, and this view was held not only by men but also by a majority of women. On the other hand, women were seen as providing a unique and essential moral influence on society through their role as mothers and homemakers. While the husband provided the economic security of the family, the wife instilled the virtues that would guide future generations. The profoundly positive belief in the importance of their moral responsibilities is perhaps obscured today by the more negative economic and political limitations that were placed on nineteenth-century women. The place of the woman was clearly considered to be in the home; however, the responsibilities of marriage and motherhood were steadfastly interpreted as increasing, rather than diminishing, the authority of women.[21] By the same token, for the married woman to seek employment outside the household was considered a distinct, if sometimes necessary, evil. One social critic condemned the increasing

139. *Drs. Starkey and Palen's Compound Oxygen.* c. 1890. Lithograph. 3⅞ x 5¾. Author's collection.

140. *The Eureka Health Corset.* c. 1880. Lithograph. 5 x 3. The Warshaw Collection of Business Americana, Smithsonian Institution.

employment of housewives in factory work as ". . . a crime to her offspring, and logically, a crime to the State, and the sooner law and sentiment make it impossible for her to stand at the loom, the sooner the character of mill operatives will be elevated."[22] The actual number of women employed in factory work remained relatively small in the later nineteenth century and was limited for the most part to recent immigrants.

As with many household items promoted today, those advertised on trade cards usually revealed the housewife as she saw herself. Regardless of the product, it is very rare to find sex being used to sell in the manner that has become so pervasive in twentieth-century advertising. Thus, while such images might have been common on barroom posters, the enticingly curvaceous beauty who represents Drs. Starkey and Palen's Compound Oxygen (Fig. 139) is a distinct rarity among trade cards. The major exception in terms of the more or less explicit depiction of the female form was with cards featuring that infamous contraption beneath which so many nineteenth-century women suffered, the corset. Trade cards advertising women's corsets were not especially common, but those that did exist usually came directly to the point on how this device could dramatically alter the anatomy. The figure represented on a card for the Eureka Health Corset (Fig. 140) might seem like an extraordinary exaggeration, but period photographs confirm that in at least some

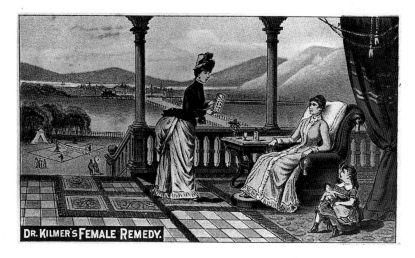

141. *Dr. and Madame Strong's Corsets.* c. 1885. Lithograph. 5½ x 2½. The Warshaw Collection of Business Americana, Smithsonian Institution.

142. *Dr. Kilmer's Female Remedy.* c. 1885. J. Ottmann, lithographers. 3 x 5⅛. The New-York Historical Society.

cases, it was not. It is remarkable that this and so many other corsets would be offered as aids to health, especially since health experts and social reformers railed against the practice of corseting throughout the century. In a classic case of deceptive advertising, one card actually claims that Doctor and Madame Strong's corsets (his is the health corset, hers the comfort corset) will "relieve the delicate and vital organs of all injurious pressure" (Fig. 141). As leading physicians pointed out at the time, corsets tended instead to damage the female anatomy and interfere with the very procreative functions these products supposedly highlighted.[23]

Women also figured prominently in trade cards advertising patent medicines, not only because they were chiefly responsible for the physical care of the family, but also because so many medicines were specifically marketed as cures for a nebulous range of "female complaints." Some of these maladies were real enough, but it must also be considered that given the generally held belief in the natural frailty of the female sex, some women were tempted to exploit

Mrs. Lydia E. Pinkham,
Of Lynn, Mass.

PUT THIS IN YOUR ALBUM.

143. *Lydia Pinkham's Vegetable Compound.* c. 1880. Engraving. 4 x 2³/₄. The New-York Historical Society.

144. *Mrs. Dinsmore's Cough and Croup Balsam.* c. 1885. Lithograph. 6¹/₂ x 4¹/₄. The Warshaw Collection of Business Americana, Smithsonian Institution.

their physical afflictions, even if unconsciously. For the sake of propriety, women suffering from such woes were usually pictured as being offered the

appropriate remedy by a concerned woman friend (Fig. 142); any male presence in such a circumstance would have been unseemly. In a further extension of such female bonds, Pinkham's Vegetable Compound had a concerted strategy of representing Mrs. Pinkham to American women as a trustworthy and sympathetic adviser. Women were encouraged to write to Mrs. Pinkham about their personal problems, and would invariably get a personal reply. An enterprising journalist eventually found that Mrs. Pinkham had died in 1883, even though letters supposedly written by her continued to be sent to customers for years afterward.[24] Lydia Pinkham's motherly portrait, which first appeared on the label of her compound in 1879, continued to be a timeless feature of the company's advertising over the decades. The message on one card bearing her portrait succinctly requests that the possessors put it in their albums (Fig. 143). Like Pinkham's Compound, Mrs. Dinsmore's cough preparation was manufactured in Lynn, Massachusetts. Perhaps inspired by the success of Pinkham's personalized advertising campaign, the promoters of this product included a portrait of its namesake—a rather stern countenance in this case—on most of the firm's trade cards. On one such card, the pictures of a number of children "saved" by Mrs. Dinsmore's balsam are arranged around her portrait (Fig. 144).

As represented in a wide variety of trade cards, the American housewife was typically young and tastefully dressed. As in so much twentieth-century advertising, the strategy clearly was to demonstrate to the average consumer that if the product was good

145. *Hires Root Beer.* c. 1890. J. Ottmann, lithographers. 5¾ x 3¾. The Warshaw Collection of Business Americana, Smithsonian Institution.

146. *Scourene.* c. 1885. Donaldson Brothers, lithographers. 4 x 5½. The Warshaw Collection of Business Americana, Smithsonian Institution.

enough for the well-to-do lady of the house, it was good enough for everybody else. From her appearance, it is rather difficult to imagine that the young mother pictured on a card for Hires' Root Beer Extract (Fig. 145) ever found it necessary to labor in the household. This upper-class mystique was further reinforced by the inclusion of household servants, whether in the form of the black nanny or butler, or the Irish house maid. A trade card for Scourene (Fig. 146) not only shows how this product can lighten the maid's cleaning chores, but suggests that her services can be dispensed with altogether. However, period sources and subsequent histories of servant labor agree that in the later nineteenth cen-

tury, the problem was a shortage rather than an overabundance of household servants. The suggestions of certain advertisements notwithstanding, it was probably the scarcity of high-quality domestic service more than anything else that encouraged the increasing adoption of household technology in America.[25] Even though the number of women engaged in domestic service almost doubled between 1870 and 1910, the demand for domestics consistently exceeded the supply.[26] In their famous manual of household management, Catherine Beecher and Harriet Beecher Stowe cited domestic service as the single greatest problem of life in America, maintaining that "the happiness of families, their thrift, well-being, and comfort, are more affected by this than by any one thing else."[27] Complaints about the lack of reliability and industry among domestic servants abounded in the late nineteenth century, but no one seemed to seriously question their necessity in a well-ordered household, particularly if, as was so frequently the case, that household contained a large number of children. Whether in the form of the professional domestic or the young woman who might spend a few years working for a friend or neighbor before her own marriage, the household servant was in fact more a commonplace of middle-class life than it was a luxury of the upper class.

Even if she was lucky enough to have domestic help, the average housewife of the later nineteenth century enjoyed few of the appliances and labor-saving devices that have done so much to lighten housework in the twentieth century. The importance of home baking has already been discussed; among the major household tasks, this was perhaps the least onerous. Even where domestic servants were employed, the lady of the house usually did most of her own cooking and baking, or at least supervised it closely. Other aspects of kitchen work were less appealing. The maintenance of even the most up-to-date coal cooking stoves took roughly an hour a day. Carrying coal and emptying ashes was heavy, dirty work, and about two hours a week had to be spent in blacking the stove to keep it from rusting.[28] When this disagreeable job was shown on trade cards for blacking or stove polishes, it was almost always being done by a black servant; in the majority of families, however, it was just one more chore for the housewife

147. *The Conqueror Wringer.* c. 1885. Donaldson Brothers, lithographers. 3¼ x 5. The Warshaw Collection of Business Americana, Smithsonian Institution.

148. *American Machine Company Irons and Fluting Machines.* c. 1885. Donaldson Brothers, lithographers. 3 x 5. The Warshaw Collection of Business Americana, Smithsonian Institution.

herself. Most oppressive of all, however, was the washing and ironing of clothing. Late nineteenth-century washing machines were very primitive appliances that frequently damaged clothing. Still a primarily manual labor, clothes washing was the task most likely to be assigned to domestic servants or sent out to washerwomen. An indication of the lowly nature of this job can be seen in the fact that while the overall majority of household domestics were white, the overwhelming majority of laundresses were black.[29] Ironing the clothes was not much less burdensome. Like washing, it was hired out when finances permitted; for housewives that had to do all their own ironing, it could occupy an entire day of the work week.[30] Trade cards for washing machines, irons, and other laundry products made little attempt to portray as glamorous duties that in reality were so odious. If they showed such activities at all, they tried to put the best face on things by claiming that technology could at least lighten these chores somewhat. Interestingly, trade cards for both the Conqueror Wringer (Fig. 147) and the fluting machines and irons of the American Machine Company (Fig. 148) show groups of housewives going about these tasks together. As early as the 1870s, Beecher and Stowe had gone a step further, suggesting that if a dozen families could pool their resources in fitting out a common laundry, "one or two women could do in first rate style what now is very indifferently done by the disturbance and disarrangement of all other domestic processes in these families."[31]

In terms of sheer numbers, all other categories of

imagery paled by comparison to the extraordinary frequency with which children were depicted on trade cards. In a general sense, this can be attributed to the almost cult status of childhood among the middle class in late nineteenth-century America. Changing attitudes toward children had already become apparent quite early in the century, when significant reappraisals of American family life began to be made. In the 1830s and 1840s, American writers produced a great number of books dealing with the rearing and education of children, sometimes with a strong religious orientation, and often with a special emphasis on the responsibilities of the mother. This "nurture literature" increased even more markedly after the Civil War. Although families remained large by twentieth-century standards, increasing economic prosperity enabled parents to devote more attention to the proper raising of children, and by the end of the century there was a vast body of literature to assist them.[32] Even more dramatic was the increasing prevalence of children in popular literature and the visual arts. The nineteenth century was the great age of the child portrait in painting, and nowhere more than in America. In the work of authors such as Charles Dickens and Mark Twain, to name only two of the more conspicuous examples, child protagonists took on an importance unparalleled in previous literature. In America, perhaps the most important development with regard to the welfare of children was the progress made in education, especially in the years after 1880. Undoubtedly inspired in part by its democratic traditions, America led the way in elementary-education reform, providing quality education for

149. *Cushman's Menthol Inhaler.* c. 1885. Richmond Lithographic Company, lithographers. 5 x 3¼. Author's collection.

girls as well as boys.

The high level of literacy among American children in the late nineteenth century is evident in the dramatic growth that took place in the publication of

150. *Scott's Emulsion.* 1889. Knapp and Company, lithographers. 5¼ x 3⅜. Author's collection.

children's books, many of which were exquisitely illustrated in color. For children exposed to such books, brightly colored trade cards were naturally a great attraction as well. Yet it is likely that in many instances, trade cards were more a part of the child's

151. *Dr. Price's Floral Riches Cologne.* c. 1870. Lithograph. 5¼ x 3¼. Author's collection.

visual experience than illustrated books. Ultimately, children were probably even more avid collectors of trade cards than adults, and for that reason alone, it is not surprising that children figured so prominently in trade card imagery. Significantly, the advertising messages on the backs of trade cards were sometimes addressed to children as well, even though they were usually not the ones who actually purchased the product in question. The back of the card for Magnetized Food illustrated in Figure 70 tells the "lively little card collector" to take this card home to show to mother, and goes on to explain that, as children's medicine, this is tasty and "far better for their health than nasty pills, oils, and powders." Given examples such as this, it is clear that just as with television commercials today, children were far from immune to high-pressure advertising; frequently they were the targeted audience. Overall, children were used to promote a much wider range of products in nineteenth-century advertising than they are today. The case of the small girl pleading with mother to take Cushman's Menthol Inhaler to bed with her (Fig. 149) is typical of the sentimental message of a host of other products.

On the positive side, there is no doubt that for many children trade cards also served a genuine educational role. For those who were just beginning to read, the back of one card for Merrick's Thread provided an alphabet in capital letters. A great number of trade cards helped acquaint youngsters with aspects of history, natural science, and geography that they might not have learned in school. Predictably, images of children from exotic places were very popular,

152. *Hoyt's German Cologne.* c. 1890.
Lithograph. 4¹/₂ x 2¹/₈. Author's
collection.

153. *Scott's Emulsion.* c. 1890. Knapp and Company,
lithographers. 4³/₄ x 3³/₄. Author's collection.

154. *Hires Root Beer.* c. 1890. Lithograph. 5 x 3.
The Warshaw Collection of Business Americana,
Smithsonian Institution.

155. *Milwaukee Harvester Company.* c. 1890. J. Ottmann, lithographers. 6¼ x 4⅛. Author's collection.

*May genial Christmas thy young heart attune
To joys as sweet as those of sunny June!*

156. *Schwartz's Toy Emporium, Boston.* 1886. Lithograph. 4 x 5⅜. Author's collection.

although sometimes, as in the case of "The Little Turk" pictured on a card for Scott's Emulsion (Fig. 150), they were distinctly idealized. The Singer Sewing Machine Company issued a large series of cards picturing the diverse peoples of the world, with each nationality shown putting the widely exported Singer machine to industrious use in making their indigenous costumes. Several of the highly competitive coffee companies issued huge numbered sets that treated educational subjects in a truly encyclopedic manner. The Arbuckle Coffee Company offered several fifty-card sets featuring topics such as animals, the history of the United States, and views from a trip around the world. The most massive single series was one issued by the McLaughlin Coffee Company, which included 225 different cards illustrating scenes of children's life. It goes without saying that these cards showed children engaged in pleasurable but consistently wholesome and constructive activities.[33]

In a society more inclined than our own to think in terms of all-encompassing symbolism, the child inevitably became a symbol of innocence, delicacy, and, in specific reference to the needs of advertising, purity.

157. *Lavine (Hartford Chemical Works).* c. 1885. Lithograph. 4 x 2¼. The Warshaw Collection of Business Americana, Smithsonian Institution.

158. *Horlick's Malted Milk.* c. 1890. Forbes Co., lithographers. 5 x 3¾. Author's collection.

159. *Nelson, Morris and Company.* c. 1895. Lithograph. 3½ x 5¾ (unextended). The Warshaw Collection of Business Americana, Smithsonian Institution.

Thus it is that children were a dominant motif on trade cards advertising soaps and food products of the sort discussed earlier. They were especially common on cards advertising colognes, perfumes, and other toiletries. Like certain other early examples, a card for Dr. Price's toilet waters and "Toothene" dentifrice (Fig. 151) shows a marked resemblance to the fancy valentines that began to become popular after

midcentury, many of which also pictured children. Hoyt's German Cologne, which was among the most lavish advertisers of its kind in the later nineteenth century, almost invariably represented children on its trade cards, often quite imaginatively. One such card showing a bespectacled infant doubles as a bookmark (Fig. 152). As indicated on the card for Dr. Price's products, purveyors of colognes and perfumes frequently scented their cards as a further inducement to the customer. On the cards for products that were intended for or particularly enjoyed by them, children were naturally a prevalent feature. Scott's Emulsion, which advertised heavily in all the advertising media and was probably the most widely used children's medication, issued a number of beautifully printed cards that were essentially portraits of children. Perhaps such adorable and contented youths as the blue-eyed "Our Boy" (Fig. 153) were an

WARNER.

FOR DIRECTIONS SEE OTHER SIDE.

FOR DIRECTIONS SEE OTHER SIDE.

160. *Dr. Warner's Perfection Waists.* c. 1890. Lithograph. 5¹/₂ x 6¹/₂. The Warshaw Collection of Business Americana, Smithsonian Institution.

attempt to gloss over the fact that Scott's Emulsion was undoubtedly the bane of existence for many a child in the late nineteenth century. On the other hand, judging from the frequency with which endearing children were shown on its trade cards, Hires' Root Beer must have been exceedingly popular with its younger consumers. Like those advertising Scott's Emulsion, the cards for Hires were exceptionally well printed. In one case, the reference to the product is cleverly placed in the fine print of a little girl's newspaper hat (Fig. 154). This highly sentimental view of children was not limited to trade cards for products that specifically pertained to them. For example, we find similar treatment on a card advertising a product as seemingly incongruous as harvesting machinery (Fig. 155).

The product intended most specifically for children was of course toys. Toymaking as a large-scale industry developed only in the nineteenth century. As with children's books, the diversity of toys that became available by the late nineteenth century is an indication of the growing prestige, and by extension the economic significance, of children in this period. Yet while children's toys were produced by a number of large manufactories, trade cards advertising them are quite rare. More common are the cards distributed by individual toy stores in the larger cities, such as the delightful and elegantly printed holiday greeting card advertising Schwartz's Toy Emporium in Boston, dating from 1886 (Fig. 156). In the last years of the century, several advertisers further exploited the popularity of trade cards among children by making simple toys and games out of the

161. *Babbitt's "1776" Soap Powder.* c. 1885. Bufford Company, lithographers. 4 x 5³⁄₈. The Warshaw Collection of Business Americana, Smithsonian Institution.

162. *Warner's Safe Yeast.* c. 1885. Mensing and Stecher, lithographers. 4 x 5³⁄₈. The Warshaw Collection of Business Americana, Smithsonian Institution.

163. *Jayne's Expectorant.* c. 1890. Knapp Company, lithographers. 4³⁄₄ x 3³⁄₄. Author's collection.

cards themselves. There was a great variety of die-cut cards in the shapes of animals, such as the widely distributed cat for Lavine cleanser (Fig. 157). Die-cut cards were often remarkably elaborate; on one card for Horlick's Malted Milk, the dairy cow actually projects outward from the milkmaid in the background (Fig. 158). Some trade cards had simple moving parts; such cards, known as mechanicals, are now especially prized by collectors. A particularly curious example is the pig distributed by a Chicago lard manufacturer that reveals an additional message when its string tail is pulled (Fig. 159). In addition to the numerous die-cut cards, some companies issued cards from which children could cut highly detailed paper dolls (Fig. 160).

Children represented on trade cards were usually shown at happy and innocent play, whether sledding down a hill in boxes of Babbitt's Soap Powder (Fig. 161) or observing the passing of a comet through a telescope fashioned from a gigantic box of Warner's Safe Yeast (Fig. 162). Yet one of the great ironies with respect to the image of childhood in the later nineteenth century is that at the very time when they were being placed on such a pedestal in popular literature and illustration, many children were in reality being exposed to unprecedented abuses as part of the industrial labor force.[34] Even on those very rare occasions when the reality of children afflicted by poverty was addressed in trade card imagery, it was in a highly sentimentalized manner. In the case of one card for

Jayne's Expectorant representing "The Beggar Children" (Fig. 163), the message on the back mentions that this scene "illustrates types of poverty which never fail to appeal, all the world over, to the kindliest feelings of our human nature." It would seem that as long as children were begging on the street rather than working long shifts in factories or coal mines, they could still be poignantly edifying to the moral

"WHY DOESN'T YOUR MAMMA WASH YOU WITH FAIRY SOAP?"
Made only by THE N. K. FAIRBANK COMPANY.
CHICAGO, ST.LOUIS, NEW YORK, BOSTON, PHILADELPHIA, PITTSBURGH, BALTIMORE.

164. *Fairbank's Fairy Soap.* 1898. Lithograph.
5 x 3¼. The Warshaw Collection of Business
Americana, Smithsonian Institution.

· LA NICHEE · (THE NEST)

165. *Scott's Emulsion.* 1887.
G. H. Buek and Company,
lithographers. 3¾ x 4¾.
The Warshaw Collection
of Business Americana,
Smithsonian Institution.

concerns of Victorian society. In regard to racial attitudes, one must wonder about the extent to which trade card imagery reinforced the same biases and ethical blind spots in children that it did in adults.

For example, the widely reproduced image copyrighted by the Fairbank Soap Company, in which a white child asks its timid and tattered black counterpart, "Why doesn't your mamma wash you with Fairy Soap?," is perhaps more insidious as a racial comment than other, more blatantly farcical stereotypes (Fig. 164).

Ultimately, the image of children as presented on trade cards is not as consistent as it might first appear. While it is true that in the vast majority of cases the innocence and purity of youth were emphasized, cer-tain others, such as the languorous young girl on a card for Scott's Emulsion (Fig. 165), seem rather ambiguous in this respect. Beyond this, there are numerous instances, particularly in the realm of clothing advertisements, where children are pre-sented almost as miniature adults. As seen in the example of the paper dolls for Dr. Warner's Perfec-tion Waists cited above (Fig. 160) and in any number of similar products (Fig. 166), children were often forced into the same kinds of stays and corsets that their parents subjected themselves to. Again, this

166. *Belvedere Shirt Waists.* c. 1885. Lithograph. 4¹/₂ x 3¹/₂. The Warshaw Collection of Business Americana, Smithsonian Institution.

167. *Boston One-Price Clothing House.* c. 1890. Lithograph. 7¹/₂ x 5¹/₂. The Warshaw Collection of Business Americana, Smithsonian Institution.

practice was widely criticized by reforming spirits, who justifiably argued that the overdressing of children placed undue pressures and complications upon them.[35] Examples like the large card issued by one clothing retailer (Fig. 167) show the extent to which the flamboyant dress fashions of the later nineteenth century carried over to the attire of children. Even if this is an extreme case, trade cards repeatedly put none-too-subtle pressure on parents to dress their children stylishly. Perhaps to an even greater extent than with adult clothing, the attire of children was viewed as a mark of upper-class respectability, and nowhere is this seen so clearly as in trade card advertising.

THE DEMISE OF THE TRADE CARD

The variety of illustrated trade cards issued by various manufacturers on the occasion of the World's Columbian Exposition, held in Chicago in 1893, would seem to indicate that the use of this medium was still as central to the advertising industry as it had been during its heyday in the 1880s. Yet there were already clear indications that the trade card was declining in its popularity among leading advertisers, and it would be very few years before the chromolithographed trade card would virtually disappear. A number of developments contributed to the ultimate extinction of the trade card, but the enormous changes that took place in periodical publishing during the late 1880s and early 1890s undoubtedly represent one of the most important factors. New postal regulations adopted in 1885 reduced the cost of second-class mailings to a flat one cent per pound. This had the immediate effect of bringing a number of new subscription-based periodicals into the field. Between 1880 and 1890, the number of monthly magazines increased by 93 percent, a much larger rate of growth than that seen in daily or weekly periodicals. By 1900, 160 leading monthlies had an average circulation of about 157,000, or roughly one-and-a-half annual subscriptions for every family in the United States.[1]

In this same period, the actual size of the general monthlies also increased dramatically. With lower postal rates, it became more profitable for publishers to provide more pages for the use of advertisers. In the decade of the 1880s, the amount of advertising that appeared in the major monthlies increased by between 200 and 300 percent. In their December 1891 issue, *Century* carried 150 pages of advertising and *Harper's Monthly* 177 pages.[2] Individual advertisers increasingly took entire pages in the monthlies; the visual appeal of these larger advertisements was greatly enhanced by the photographs and other illustrations made possible with the widespread commercial application of halftone printing in the later 1890s. True color printing for mass-magazine publication was still not very common at this point; the three-color printing process that would become a standard technique of the industry was generally available to the magazine publishers only after 1900. However, certain enterprising advertisers, led by Ivory Soap in 1896, commissioned full-color lithographic prints that were sent directly from specialty printers to the publishers, who would bind them into the magazines.[3] These lithographed inserts were large enough for framing, and the quality of printing was excellent. As with trade cards, advertising messages often appeared on the backs of these insert prints. By commissioning an insert in a major magazine, the advertiser could be assured of reaching literally hundreds of thousands of families within a given month.

Given the versatility and extraordinary popularity of the illustrated magazine around the end of the century, it is not surprising that companies that had traditionally been heavy advertisers turned increasingly to this medium. Perhaps more significantly, however, many new products in the 1890s used the illustrated magazine almost exclusively for their advertising. The case of bicycles has already been mentioned. Other new products widely advertised in magazines included typewriters, cameras, and electrical products (particularly those of the Edison Company). Also, by the late 1890s a much greater variety of processed food products was being marketed than in the 1880s. In its approach to advertising, the case of the National Biscuit Company is particularly instructive. Founded in 1898, this company immediately set out to convince consumers to buy a product called Uneeda Biscuit, a type of soda cracker sold in a patented airtight package. The advertising campaign consisted primarily of posters and saturation coverage in newspapers and magazines, including colored inserts. Although drummers flooded the backwoods market with buttons and other trinkets, the company never made use of trade cards. Innovative packaging and advertising together created such a demand that within a matter of months, the company actually ceased advertising temporarily in order to catch up with back orders. Soon there were so many sound-alike imitators on the market that National Biscuit Company took legal action against them.[4] One major exception to the general trend toward intensive magazine advertising in the 1890s was the patent medicine business. Patent medicine makers would undoubtedly have been as eager to advertise in the major monthly magazines as anyone else. However, in 1892, Cyrus Curtis announced that the *Ladies' Home Journal* would no longer accept patent medicine advertising; this same magazine launched an all-out campaign against the industry in 1904. That many other family magazines also eliminated patent medicine advertising had to do not only with the obvious abuses perpetrated by this industry, but also with the abundance of other manufacturing interests clamoring for advertising space. Publishers like Curtis scarcely needed to worry about any loss of revenue from the likes of Pinkham's Vegetable Compound.

Along with changes in the categories of products most heavily advertised, one must also consider the fact that by the 1890s monopolistic practices in American business had become more pronounced than ever before. Many of the competitors in food products, household goods, and any number of other industries that had advertised with trade cards in the 1870s and 1880s had progressively been weeded out. To a greater

extent than ever before, the management, and therefore the advertising organization, of American consumer industries was being centralized in the urban northeast. Of the 2,583 general advertisers that were using American periodicals in 1898, two-thirds were located in the northeast, and fully one-third were in New York State alone.[5] Magazine advertising provided these advertisers with a nationwide audience that did not require the intermediary that the distribution of trade cards generally did. Indeed, advertisements in illustrated magazines, together with increasingly monopolistic concentrations in industry, had a great deal to do with the gradual disappearance of what had been the primary purveyor of trade cards, the commercial traveler. The tendency in the 1890s was clearly toward using printed matter, shipped together with order blanks and samples, in place of the personal contact of the drummer. By the end of the century, a number of large manufacturers had completely dispensed with commercial travelers, selling only by catalog directly to retailers.[6]

The small local retailer, who had been the final distributor of most trade cards to the consuming public, also began to be threatened by changing marketing practices around the end of the century. General store merchants in small towns that were close to cities already had to compete with the attractions of the large department stores. However, that competition was minor compared to the more general threat posed by the development of mail-order houses. Aaron Montgomery Ward started in Chicago with next to nothing in 1872; ten years later, his catalog contained nearly ten thousand items. His success was

based simply on buying large quantities of goods directly from manufacturers and in turn selling them for cash to the consumer through his catalogs. Having himself been a commercial traveler in dry goods in the Midwest, Ward thoroughly understood the limitations and problems farmers had in dealing with small general stores. From the beginning, Ward aimed particularly at the rural customer and worked closely with Grange organizations to establish his credibility with farmers.[7] When Richard Sears entered the mail-order business in the 1880s, he appealed to this same rural market. The growth of Sears's company was even more meteoric, largely because of his relentless advertising in periodicals. Advertising for mail-order businesses was so heavy in some rural journals that these soon became known as "mail order magazines." To fully understand the threat of giant mail-order houses to the small general store owner, it must be considered that they offered far more than dry goods at bargain prices. For example, grocery products were for a time the leading group in dollar volume for Sears. In 1896, the Sears Roebuck catalog even began listing some of the more popular patent medicines.[8] In a remarkably short time, the mail-order houses brought about a complete revolution in the buying habits of rural and small-town America. Their position in this market was enhanced all the more by the institution of Rural Free Delivery, which was begun on a rather haphazard basis in 1893. With this, most rural families were able to receive mail directly at their residence instead of journeying into town. (Traditionally, many rural post offices had been located in general stores, making the local populace that much more dependent on them.) Although small-town merchants fought it bitterly for years, when the United States Postal Service began offering free parcel delivery on rural routes after 1900, the fate of the general store was virtually sealed.[9] And, just as the big mail-order houses progressively ruined many small retailers, so too did their lavishly illustrated catalogues eliminate the functional need for trade cards as a source of product information.

Another innovation in advertising techniques that eventually undermined the use of trade cards was the illustrated post card. Post cards had existed in America from the time that the government issued the first penny postals in 1873. For many years, however, advertising post cards were used primarily by local retailers to contact a limited clientele, sometimes to inform them of the arrival of goods or of special sales. Such illustration as existed on these cards usually consisted of a view of the business premises or of the goods it offered, not unlike what is frequently found on the reverse side of lithographed trade cards. Illustration was almost always in black and white and usually of rather poor quality.[10] However, as a means of direct advertising, the post card soon proved to be extremely effective. In 1892, Richard Sears sent out eight thousand postal cards with imitation handwriting printed from zinc plates. He received two thousand orders in return, at a cost of less than five cents per order.[11]

Not until the later 1890s did the use of post cards catch on as a truly popular and nationwide phenomenon. This also was due in large part to the reduced cost and general improvement of postal service. In 1898, postal regulations were changed to allow privately printed post cards the same message privileges and postal rates as the government-issue cards. That change heralded the full-color picture post cards purchased by the millions in America after the turn of the century. It also permitted the development of advertising cards that carried illustration on one side and further printed information on the other. Aside from the space for stamp and addressee, this format was essentially the same as that of late nineteenth-century trade cards. Advertising manuals published in the 1890s increasingly recommended the medium of post cards for their low cost and direct communication with the consumer. Significantly, these same manuals did not even mention the use of traditional trade cards.[12] The post card had the obvious advantage of allowing advertisers to target specific consumer groups at any time they wished. As in the case of Sears's highly successful experiment, it could also be used by the consumer to respond directly to the advertiser. Even more than periodical advertising, the advertising post card succeeded in rendering the traditional trade card obsolete by the beginning of the twentieth century.

Although the lithographers themselves were seldom identified, the printing quality of some advertising post cards lithographed in color around the end of the nineteenth century was by no means inferior to that of trade cards. A card for Bensdorp's Royal Dutch Cocoa (Fig. 168) is one in their series of advertising post cards that shows exceptionally sophisticated color printing. As with many earlier trade

168. *Bensdorp's Royal Dutch Cocoa.* c. 1900. Lithographed advertising post card. $5^{1}/_{2}$ x $3^{1}/_{2}$. Collection of Richard Taylor.

"HATCHED IN A SUCCESSFUL"

Compliments of the

Des Moines Incubator Company

DES MOINES IOWA

Catalog Free

169. *Des Moines Incubator Company.* c. 1910. Half-tone advertising post card. 3½ x 5½. Author's collection.

cards, there is a space for the imprinting of a local dealership at the bottom. Admittedly, such high-quality color lithography was much more the exception than the rule among advertising post cards. More typical were the post cards illustrated by means of halftone photographs, usually printed in black and white, occasionally with one or two colors added. Although they could scarcely compare with the sumptuousness of color lithography, such cards opened a wide range of possibilities for the advertising needs of large companies and small businesses alike. Their use steadily increased in the first two decades of the twentieth century and, at least in terms of local businesses, reached their peak of popularity in

the 1920s, slowly declining thereafter. Photographic printing of post cards tended to bring back the sort of highly individualized imagery that had characterized advertising in the early days of trade cards. Often advertising post cards for local businesses could be eccentric to the point of the bizarre, as with one curious card distributed by the Des Moines Incubator Company (Fig. 169). During the later nineteenth century, photographic printing on trade cards had never really caught on in America, but in Europe it was quite common and persisted for some time, especially since the advertising post card was less of a factor there.

By 1900, the lithographic industry in America had

begun to fall on hard times. With most firms, this actually had little to do with the gradual disappearance of lithographed trade cards. In many cases, the small companies that had relied on job work in cards and other small-format commissions were simply swallowed up by larger ones. Larger firms, the Strobridge Company of Cincinnati being one notable example, continued to do a thriving business in multi-colored posters, calendars, show cards, and other larger-format work. However, a major concern for American lithographic printers was the increasing competition from abroad, particularly from German printers. In a pamphlet published in 1909, the National Association of Employing Lithographers complained bitterly about the volume of cigar bands, labels, post cards, and other color work flooding in from Germany. Although tariffs on imported lithographic printing were already high, the association urged even tighter restrictions on the grounds that German lithographic workers were paid only a quarter of the salary of their American counterparts and thus represented unfair competition.[13] Regardless of differences in wages, the fact was that the quality of German lithographic printing at the beginning of the twentieth century was extremely high, perhaps even unrivaled, and this must have concerned American firms as much as any purely economic factors. Tariffs were in fact increased, although with trade cards already having virtually disappeared, the main impact was on foreign-printed postal and greeting cards. It is worth noting, however, that in the last years of the nineteenth century, some of the most exquisitely printed trade cards distributed in

170. *Liebig's Extract of Beef.* c. 1895. Lithographed calendar folder. "Printed in Bavaria." 2⁷/₈ x 4³/₄ (opened). The Warshaw Collection of Business Americana, Smithsonian Institution.

America were being imported from Europe; ten to twenty years earlier, Americans had been exporting lithographed cards, especially to Latin America and Asia. The vast variety of cards issued by the Liebig Company, purveyors of a highly successful line of prepared food extracts, represent a unique case in that the products were heavily advertised in America, England, and the European continent, and trade cards for them were printed in all of these markets. Frequently, cards advertising Liebig's Extract would be printed in one country for use in another. Although not in typical card format, the folding calendar for the year 1896, printed in Bavaria for American and possibly British distribution, gives a good indication of the remarkable standards of

lithographic printing evident with most Leibig's cards (Fig. 170). Ironically, the most expertly and beautifully printed trade cards, many of which were produced in Europe, appeared in America just as their popularity among both advertisers and the general public was waning.

Perhaps the most remarkable fact about illustrated trade cards is that while they were used to advertise every conceivable kind of product in the last quarter of the nineteenth century and were collected by millions of Americans, they also went out of fashion very rapidly and had virtually disappeared by the beginning of the twentieth century. Various kinds of cards distributed free to the consuming public might have been used in later years, but they no longer repre-

sented the popular art form and the medium of family entertainment that lithographed trade cards of the later nineteenth century had been. However, one company did continue for many years to insert small lithographed cards in packages in the manner of some of the late nineteenth-century manufacturers. Church and Company, makers of Arm and Hammer Baking Soda, have sporadically issued series of wildlife cards as premiums throughout much of the twentieth century. For many years, these cards were very well printed, and although the printer is not indicated, many are believed to have been produced by the Prang Company in Boston.[14] These cards are quite small and were clearly intended to serve an educational purpose for youthful collectors. In 1976, Arm and Hammer issued a set of cards featuring birds of prey that could be obtained with a boxtop and thirty-five cents.[15] This series was to mark the bicentennial of the American Revolution, but it also represented the centennial of the first occasion on which illustrated trade cards were introduced to the collecting public on a massive scale, the Centennial Exhibition in Philadelphia. Luckily, the fact that so many trade cards were lovingly stored away in family albums in the later nineteenth century has meant that at least a portion of this otherwise ephemeral art form has been preserved to be reevaluated and collected anew. This limited examination has attempted to provide the general outlines for the ongoing and virtually inexhaustible study of what has been the most diverse, but at the same time the most neglected, medium in the history of nineteenth-century American advertising.

NOTES FOR INTRODUCTION

1. Quoted in Daniel Boorstin, *The Americans: The Democratic Experience* (New York, 1973), p. 121.
2. Ernest Bogart and Donald Kemmerer, *Economic History of the American People* (New York, 1942), p. 678.
3. *The Nation* 23 (9 November 1876): 284.
4. [Edward W. Byrn], "The Progress of Invention during the Past Fifty Years," *Scientific American* 75 (25 July 1896): 82–83. Reprinted in Thomas Parke Hughes, ed., *Changing Attitudes toward American Technology* (New York, 1975), pp. 158–65.
5. "The Advertising Card Business," *The Paper World* 10 (May 1885): 5.

NOTES FOR CHAPTER 1: THE SEVENTEENTH AND EIGHTEENTH CENTURIES

1. Ambrose Heal, "Samuel Pepys—His Trade-Cards," *Connoisseur* 92 (September 1933): 165–71. See also Heal's "Seventeenth-Century Booksellers and Stationers Cards," *Alphabet and Image* 8 (1948): 51–62.
2. Heal, *London Tradesmen's Cards of the XVIII Century: An Account of Their Origin and Use* (New York, 1968), p. 1.
3. Several examples are illustrated in Dorothy O. Shilton and Richard Holworthy, "Old London Bill-Headings," *Connoisseur* 66 (August 1923): 205–14.
4. John Lewis, *Printed Ephemera* (Ipswich, 1962), p. 174. Lewis points out that on many cards of this period, wood engraving was used to imitate metal type.
5. Heal, *London Tradesmen's Cards,* pp. 38–62.
6. Heal, *The London Furniture Makers, from the Restoration to the Victorian Era, 1660–1840* (London, 1953); *The London Goldsmiths, 1200–1800* (London, 1935). In this context, see also Keith Neal and D. H. L. Back, *British Gunmakers: Their Trade Cards, Cases and Equipment, 1760–1860* (Warminster, 1980), which is documented with a number of eighteenth-century trade cards.
7. Heal, *London Tradesmen's Cards,* p. 80.
8. Ibid., p. 70.
9. See John Grand-Carteret, *Vieux Papiers—Vieilles Images* (Paris, 1896), and Ernest Maindron, *Les Programmes Illustrés des Théâtres et des Cafés—Concerts, Menus, Cartes d'Invitation, Petites Estampes, etc.* (Paris, 1897).
10. Sinclair H. Hitchings, "Graphic Arts in Colonial New England," in *Prints in and of America to 1850,* ed. John D. Morse (Winterthur, Del., 1970), p. 97.
11. See George Francis Dow, "Trade Cards," *Old-Time New England* 26 (April 1936): 123. Dow also illustrates Johnson's own trade card, which he dates 1732. Unfortunately, he gives no information about these cards to collaborate their dates.
12. Mary Elizabeth Means, *Early American Trade Cards* (M.A. thesis, Winterthur Program, Winterthur, Del., 1958), p. 18.
13. Charles Dexter Allen, *American Book Plates—A Guide to Their Study with Examples* (Boston, 1894), pp. 115–16.
14. Clarence S. Brigham, *Paul Revere's Engravings* (New York, 1969), pp. 174–75. Brigham lists five cards by Revere in the collection of the American Antiquarian Society. There were also two later trade cards advertising Revere and Son in the Landauer Collection of the New-York Historical Society, but both are now missing. See Means, *Early American Trade Cards,* pp. 23–24.
15. Arthur J. Pulos, *American Design Ethic* (Cambridge, Mass., 1983), p. 27.
16. Brigham, *Paul Revere's Engravings,* p. 169. The other card to which Brigham refers was for the Boston merchant William Jackson and is now held by the Metropolitan Museum. The Jackson card lacks the signature found on the bottom right of the Breck card.
17. Allen, *American Book Plates,* pp. 127–32.
18. The Warner card is illustrated in Heal, *London Tradesmen's Cards,* plate 80.
19. Allen, *American Book Plates,* p. 129.
20. Fiske Kimball, "The Sources of the Philadelphia Chippendale, II: Benjamin Randolph's Trade Card," *The Pennsylvania Museum Bulletin* 23 (October 1927): 5–8.
21. Harrold E. Gillingham, "Old Business Cards of Philadelphia," *Pennsylvania Magazine of History and Biography* 53 (July 1929): 204.
22. Means, *Early American Trade Cards,* p. 42. On early illustrated newspaper advertisements, see Kenneth Scott, "Advertising Woodcuts in Colonial Newspapers," *Antiques* 67 (February 1955): 152–53.
23. Adele Jenny, *Early American Trade Cards from the Collection of Bella C. Landauer* (New York, 1927), p. 11. This card has been reproduced in several places, but beyond Jenny's brief discussion, little has been said about it.

NOTES FOR CHAPTER 2: EVOLUTION IN THE NINETEENTH CENTURY

1. See Dow, "Trade Cards," pp. 129, 132.
2. See the various reproductions in Allen, *American Book Plates.* Most of the plates Allen discusses are from the eighteenth century, but he illustrates enough early-nineteenth-century examples to show this general evolution.
3. Illustrated in Stephen Dewitt Stephens, *The Mavericks: American Engravers* (New Brunswick, N.J., 1950), following p. 76 (plate no. 1017).
4. Scoles's personal trade card is also in the collection of the New-York Historical Society. On the Rollinson card, see Means, *Early American Trade Cards,* p. 187, fig. 44.
5. See Means, *Early American Trade Cards,* p. 200, fig. 59.
6. On America's debt to European lithographic technology, see Peter Marzio, *The Democratic Art: Pictures for a Nineteenth-Century America* (Boston, 1979), pp. 64–73.
7. Marzio, "American Lithographic Technology," in *Prints in and of America,* ed. Morse, p. 222.
8. Reproduced in Alice E. Ford, "Some Trade Cards and Broadsides," *American Collector* 11 (June 1942): 10.
9. Marzio, *The Democratic Art,* p. 43.
10. This publication, also known as the *Manual of the Corporation of the City of New York,* ed. David Thomas Valentine, appeared from the early 1840s until 1870. Beginning in 1864, the *Manual* was printed by Major and Knapp.
11. The Philadelphia directory was first published in 1794. On early Philadelphia architectural lithographs, see in particular Nicolas Wainwright, *Philadelphia in the Romantic Age of Lithography* (Philadelphia, 1958).
12. Ibid., p. 70.
13. Illustrated in Marzio, *The Democratic Art,* p. 25. A copy of this brochure is in the collection of the New York Public Library.

14. Wainwright, *Philadelphia in the Romantic Age of Lithography*, p. 86.

15. On clipper ship cards, see the thorough study by Allan Forbes, "The Story of Clipper Ship Sailing Cards," *Proceedings, American Antiquarian Society* 59 (October 1949): 225–74; also, Willard Emerson Keyes, "Yankee Clipper Cards," *Antiques* 33 (March 1938): 128–31.

16. Katherine Morrison McClinton, *The Chromolithographs of Louis Prang* (New York, 1973), p. 4.

17. Ibid., p. 32.

18. Marzio, *The Democratic Art*, p. 90.

19. Prang's own account of his development of advertising and greeting cards was published in a letter to *The Lithographer and Printer* 4 (13 June 1885): 326.

20. Jefferson R. Burdick, *The American Card Catalogue* (New York, 1967), p. 13.

NOTES TO CHAPTER 3: THE ADVERTISER AND THE TRADE CARD

1. Boorstin, *The Americans*, pp. 137–38.

2. See, for example, "Art and Advertising," *The Nation* 20 (20 May 1875): 342–43.

3. "Printers' Ink: Fifty Years, 1888–1938," *Printers' Ink* 184 (28 July 1938): 33.

4. Frank Luther Mott, *A History of American Magazines* (Cambridge, Mass., 1957), 3:10.

5. Ibid., p. 9.

6. Quoted in Marzio, *The Democratic Art*, p. 99.

7. See John Wilmerding, *Important Information Inside: The Art of John F Peto and the Idea of Still-life Painting in Nineteenth-Century America* (Washington, D.C., 1983), pp. 206, 212.

8. Burdick, *The American Card Catalogue*, pp. 17–18.

9. Bella Landauer has claimed that the price for Currier and Ives trade cards was six dollars a hundred. If that figure is accurate, their cards were considerably more expensive than those of their major competitors. See Landauer's "Some Trade Cards with Particular Emphasis on the Currier and Ives Contributions," *Quarterly, New York Historical Society*, January 1934, p. 87.

10. On the use of cosmetics in nineteenth-century America, see the excellent discussion in Lois W. Banner's *American Beauty* (Chicago, 1983), pp. 40–44.

11. Frank Presbrey, *The History and Development of Advertising* (New York, 1929), p. 362. As late as 1898, medicines and remedies still accounted for more than twice as much periodical advertising as any other class of product. This statistic is all the more remarkable considering that several leading magazines, including *Ladies Home Journal*, had by this time banned patent medicines from their advertising columns.

12. Sidney A. Sherman, "Advertising in the United States," *Publications of the American Statistical Association* 7 (December 1900): 37.

13. On the relation between prevalent diseases and advertising strategies of the patent medicine trade, see James H. Young, *The Toadstool Millionaires* (Princeton, N.J., 1961), pp. 157ff.

14. George P. Rowell, *The Men who Advertise. An Account of Successful Advertisers together with Hints on the Method of Advertising* (New York, 1870), p. 32.

15. John S. Haller and Robin M. Haller, *The Physician and Sexuality in Victorian America* (Urbana, Ill., 1974), p. 289.

16. Ibid., p. 285.

17. Harold Barger, *Distribution's Place in the American Economy since 1869* (Princeton, N.J., 1955), p. 131.

18. On the popularity of Jumbo in trade card imagery, see the article by Bella Landauer, "Jumbo's Influence on Advertising, or some Jumbo Trade-Cards," *Quarterly, New York Historical Society*, October 1934, pp. 45–52.

19. Grace Rogers Cooper, *The Invention of the Sewing Machine* (Washington, D.C., 1968), p. 65. This remains the definitive account of the early history of the sewing machine. Pages 65–74 give a full listing of the makers and their years of production.

20. "Home, and the Sewing Machine," *National Magazine* 12 (June 1858): 543.

21. Harvey Green, *The Light of the Home* (New York, 1983), p. 82.

22. Ibid., p. 83.

23. Lawrence Johnson, *Over the Counter and on the Shelf: Country Storekeeping in America, 1620–1920* (Rutland, Vt., 1961), p. 101.

24. "Printers' Ink: Fifty Years," p. 23.

25. Edward C. Hampe and Merle Wittenberg, *The Lifeline of America: The Development of the Food Industry* (New York, 1964), p. 130.

26. Presbrey, *History and Development of Advertising*, p. 386.

27. Susan Strasser, *Never Done: A History of American Housework* (New York, 1982), pp. 23–24.

28. Green, *The Light of the Home*, p. 61.

29. "Printers' Ink: Fifty Years," p. 24.

30. Arnold B. Barach, *Famous American Trademarks* (Washington, D.C., 1971), p. 7.

31. On this subject, see Josephine Peirce, *Fire on the Hearth: The Evolution and Romance of the Heating Stove* (Springfield, Mass., 1951).

32. Russell Lynes, *The Domesticated Americans* (New York, 1963), pp. 140–43.

33. Fred A. Shannon, *The Farmer's Last Frontier: Agriculture, 1860–1897* (New York, 1968), p. 139. On the development of American agricultural machinery, see Leo Rogin, *The Introduction of Farm Machinery in Its Relation to the Productivity of Labor in the Agriculture of the United States during the Nineteenth Century* (Berkeley, University of California Publications in Economics, vol. 9, 1931).

34. Nathan Rosenberg, *Technology and American Economic Growth* (White Plains, N.Y., 1972), p. 89.

35. Mott, *A History of American Magazines*, 4:24.

NOTES TO CHAPTER 4: THE MAJOR THEMES

1. Marshall McLuhan developed a perceptive study of this theme in his *Mechanical Bride* as early as 1951. A host of other studies, dealing especially with television advertising, have followed.

2. On the evolution of this and other patriotic personifications, see E. McClung Fleming, "Symbols of the United States: From Indian Queen to Uncle Sam," in *Frontiers of American Culture*, ed. Ray B. Browne et al. (West Lafayette, Ind., 1968), pp. 1–24.

3. Ibid., p. 20.

4. Alec Davis, *Package into Print* (London, 1968), p. 82.

5. Cited in Roy Ginger, *The Age of Excess: The United States from 1877 to 1914* (New York, 1965), p. 74.

6. See for example Edward Perry, *The Image of the Indian and the Black Man in American Art, 1590–1900* (New York, 1974). On these minorities in popular literature, Charles R. Wilson's "Racial Reservations: Indians and Blacks in American Magazines, 1865–1900," *Journal of Popular Culture* 10 (Summer 1976): 70–79, provides a short but illuminating discussion.

7. Fleming, "Symbols of the United States," pp. 1–2.

8. Bella Landauer's privately published booklet on this theme, *The Indian Does Not Vanish in American Advertising* (New York, 1940), deals with the subject in reference to her own rich collection of trade cards.

9. Ronald T. Takaki, *Iron Cages: Race and Culture in Nineteenth-Century America* (New York, 1979), p. 174.

10. On some of the stories associated with the origins of supposed Indian remedies, see Young, *The Toadstool Millionaires*, pp. 176–77.

11. Ginger, *The Age of Excess*, p. 77.

12. Takaki, *Iron Cages*, pp. 232–39.

13. Ibid., p. 216.

14. See Bella Landauer's privately printed pamphlet, *Gilbert and Sullivan Influences on American Tradecards, from the Collection of Bella C. Landauer* (New York, 1936).

15. Alan Trachtenberg, *The Incorporation of America: Culture and Society in the Gilded Age* (New York, 1982), p. 134.

16. Lewis Atherton, *Main Street on the Middle Border* (Bloomington, Ind., 1954), pp. 230–31.

17. Trachtenberg, *The Incorporation of America*, p. 139. Trachtenberg states, "The denial of the labor of its audience is thus of prime importance to the mode of the advertisement, a corollary to its denial of the labor represented in its goods." Given the frequent references to the factory in trade card advertising, this distinction would seem to be less appropriate to the nineteenth than to the twentieth century.

18. Green, *The Light of the Home*, p. 143.

19. Henry Nash Smith, *Virgin Land: The American West as Symbol and Myth* (Cambridge, Mass., 1970), p. 159. On the promotion of the West as an area for settlement, see also Katherine B. Clinton, "The New West: Themes in Nineteenth-Century Urban Promotion, 1815–1880," *Bulletin of the Missouri Historical Society* 30 (January 1974): 75–88.

20. Cited in Strasser, *Never Done*, p. 244.

21. On the literature supporting these sentiments, see in particular Barbara Welter, *Dimity Convictions: The American Woman*

in the Nineteenth Century (Athens, Ohio, 1976), pp. 38–41.

22. Carroll D. Wright, "The Factory as an Element in Civilization," *Journal of Social Science* 16 (December 1882); reprinted in Sigmond Diamond, ed., *The Nation Transformed* (New York, 1963), p. 49.

23. Green, *The Light of the Home*, p. 122.

24. Young, *The Toadstool Millionaires*, pp. 213–14.

25. On this point, see Faye E. Dudden, *Serving Women: Household Service in Nineteenth-Century America* (Middletown, Conn., 1983), p. 127.

26. David M. Katzman, *Seven Days a Week: Women and Domestic Service in Industrializing America* (New York, 1978), p. 46. The actual increase was from 960,000 in 1870 to 1,830,000 in 1910.

27. Catherine Beecher and Harriet Beecher Stowe, *Principles of Domestic Science* (New York, 1871), p. 276.

28. Strasser, *Never Done*, p. 41.

29. Katzman, *Seven Days a Week*, p. 73.

30. Green, *The Light of the Home*, p. 75.

31. Beecher and Stowe, *Principles of Domestic Science*, p. 290.

32. See for example the large bibliography in Bernard Wishy, *The Child and the Republic* (Philadelphia, 1968), pp. 182–201.

33. Burdick's *The American Card Catalogue* provides a list of the major series issued by the coffee companies on pp. 92–95.

34. On this point, see C. John Sommerville, *The Rise and Fall of Childhood* (London, 1982), pp. 160–78.

35. See Wishy, *The Child and the Republic*, p. 123, and Green, *The Light of the Home*, pp. 43–44.

NOTES TO EPILOGUE

1. Sherman, "Advertising in the United States," p. 3.

2. Mott, *History of American Magazines*, 4:1.

3. Presbrey, *History and Development of Advertising*, p. 396. The Ivory Soap lithograph, printed in Cincinnati, appeared in *Leslie's Illustrated Monthly*.

4. On the Uneeda Biscuit phenomenon, see "Uneeda Biscuit," *Modern Packaging* 22 (February 1949): 82–86, 172, 174, 176; also Gerald Carson, *The Old Country Store* (New York, 1954), pp. 274–75.

5. Sherman, "Advertising in the United States," p. 141.

6. Ibid., p. 129.

7. Boorstin, *The Americans*, pp. 121–23.

8. Boris Emmet and John E. Jeuck, *Catalogues and Counters: A History of Sears, Roebuck and Company* (Chicago, 1950), p. 102.

9. Wayne Fuller, *RFD, the Changing Face of Rural America* (Bloomington, Ind., 1964), pp. 212ff.

10. On early advertising post cards, see Jefferson R. Burdick, *Pioneer Post Cards: The Story of Mailing Cards to 1898* (New York, 1964), pp. 116–33, 181, 197.

11. Emmet and Jeuck, *Catalogues and Counters*, p. 45.

12. See for example Charles A. Bates, *Good Advertising* (New York, 1896), pp. 283–84; Nathaniel C. Fowler, Jr., *Fowler's Publicity* (New York, 1897), pp. 236–37.

13. National Association of Employing Lithographers, *American Lithography; Its Growth; Its Development; Its Need of Tariff Protection* (Rochester, N.Y., 1909), p. 2. On the background of tariff regulations on imported lithographic work, see Marzio, *The Democratic Art*, pp. 90–93.

14. Larry Freeman, *Louis Prang: Color Lithographer* (Watkins Glen, N.Y., 1971), p. 40.

15. See Elizabeth Pullar, "Baking Soda Bonus Cards: Arm and Hammer Trade Cards Designed by L. A. Fuertes," *Antiques Journal* 35 (January 1980): 36–38.

1. GENERAL REFERENCE WORKS

Brown, H. Glenn, and Brown, Maude O. *A Directory of the Book-Arts and Book Trades in Philadelphia to 1820 including Painters and Engravers.* New York, 1950.

Comstock, Helen, ed. *The Concise Encyclopedia of American Antiques.* 2 vols. New York, 1958.

Ferguson, Eugene S. *Bibliography of the History of Technology.* Boston, 1968.

Fielding, Mantle. *Mantle Fielding's Dictionary of American Painters, Sculptors and Engravers.* New York, 1965.

Groce, George Cuthbert, Jr., and Wallace, David H. *The New York Historical Society's Dictionary of Artists in America, 1564–1860.* New Haven, 1957.

Josephson, Askel, compiler. *A List of Books on the History of Industry and Industrial Arts.* Chicago, 1915.

Karpel, Bernard, ed. *Arts in America. A Bibliography.* 4 vols. Washington, D.C., 1979.

Kelley, Etna. *The Business Founding Date Directory.* Scarsdale, N.Y., 1954.

Larson, Henrietta. *Guide to Business History.* Cambridge, Mass., 1948.

Lovett, Robert W. *American Economic Business History Information Sources.* Detroit, 1971.

Ludman, Joan, and Mason, Lauris. *Fine Print References: A Selected Bibliography of Print-Related Literature.* Millwood, N.Y., 1982.

McKay, George Leslie. *A Register of Artists, Engravers, Booksellers, Bookbinders, Printers and Publishers in New York City, 1633–1820.* New York, 1942.

Newberry Library. *Dictionary Catalogue of the History of Printing from the John M. Wing Foundation in the Newberry Library.* 6 vols. Boston, 1961.

Pollay, Richard W. *Information Sources in Advertising History.* Westport, Conn., 1979.

Romaine, Lawrence. *A Guide to American Trade Catalogues, 1744–1900.* New York, 1960.

Smith, Ralph Clifton. *A Bibliographical Index of American Artists.* New York, 1930.

Stauffer, David McNeely. *American Engravers upon Copper and Steel.* 2 vols. New York, 1907.

Ulrich, Carolyn E, and Kup, Karl. *Books and Printing: A Selected List of Periodicals, 1800–1942.* Woodstock, Vt., 1943.

United States Bureau of the Census. *Historical Statistics of the United States: Colonial Times to 1970.* Washington, D.C., 1975.

Young, William, ed. *A Dictionary of American Artists, Sculptors and Engravers.* Cambridge, Mass., 1968.

2. SOURCES ON THE HISTORY OF THE TRADE CARD

"A Short History of Trade Cards." *Bulletin of the Business Historical Society* 5 (April 1931): 1–6.

Book Club of California. *Early California Trade Cards.* San Francisco, 1966.

Burdick, Jefferson R. *The American Card Catalogue.* New York, 1967.

———. *Pioneer Post Cards; The Story of Mailing Cards to 1898.* New York, 1964.

Calvert, H. R. *Scientific Trade Cards in the Science Museum Collections.* London, 1971.

Cotterell, Howard H., and Heal, Ambrose. "Pewterers' Trade Cards." *Connoisseur* 76 (December 1926): 221–26; 80 (February 1928): 81–90.

Dow, George Francis. "Trade Cards." *Old-Time New England* 26 (April 1936): 115–37; 26 (July 1936): 10–22.

Forbes, Allan. "The Story of Clipper Ship Sailing Cards." *Proceedings, American Antiquarian Society* 59 (October 1949): 225–74.

Ford, Alice E. "Some Trade Cards and Broadsides." *American Collector* 11 (June 1942): 10–13.

Frank, Gerold. "Children's Nineteenth-Century Trading Cards." *Coronet* 43 (January 1958): 131–39.

Gillingham, Harrold E. "Business Cards of Early Philadelphia Merchants." *Pennsylvania Magazine of History and Biography* 53 (July 1929): 203–29.

Grade, Arnold. "Paper Mechanicals." *Americana* 5 (March 1977): 20–23.

Heal, Ambrose. "Booksellers and Stationers Trade-Cards of the Eighteenth Century." *Penrose Annual* 45 (1951): 29–32.

———. *London Tradesmen's Cards of the Eighteenth Century. An Account of Their Origin and Use.* New York, 1968.

———. "Samuel Pepys, His Trade Cards." *Connoisseur* 92 (September 1933): 165–71.

———. "Seventeenth-Century Booksellers and Stationers Trade Cards." *Alphabet and Image* 8 (1948): 31–62.

———. *The London Furniture Makers, from the Restoration to the Victorian Era, 1660–1840.* London, 1953.

———. *The London Goldsmiths, 1200–1800.* London, 1935.

———. "Trade Cards of Engravers." *Print Collectors Quarterly* 14 (July 1927): 218–50.

Jenny, Adele. *Early American Trade Cards from the Collection of Bella C. Landauer.* New York, 1927.

Keyes, Willard Emerson. "Yankee Clipper Cards." *Antiques* 33 (March 1938): 128–31.

Kimball, Fiske. "The Sources of the Philadelphia Chippendale, II: Benjamin Randolph's Trade Card." *The Pennsylvania Museum Bulletin* 23 (October 1927): 5–8.

Landauer, Bella C. *Gilbert and Sullivan Influence on American Trade Cards.* New York, 1936.

———. "Jumbo's Influence on Advertising, or some 'Jumbo' Trade Cards." *New York Historical Society Bulletin* 18 (October 1934): 45–52.

———. *Some Embossed American Trade Cards.* New York, 1941.

———. "Some Trade Cards with Particular Emphasis on the Currier and Ives Contributions." *New York Historical Society Bulletin* 17 (January 1934): 79–93.

———. *The Indian Does Not Vanish in American Advertising.* New York, 1940.

———. "Trade Cards: An Overlooked Asset." *Bulletin of the Business Historical Society* 9 (1935): 33–38.

Landauer, Bella C., and Weiss, Harry B. "Some Trade Cards of American Engravers." *American Book Collector* 4 (1933): 250–55, 308–11; 5 (1933): 16–18.

Maust, Don. "The American Trade Card." *Antiques Journal* 22 (June 1967): 24–27.

"Maverick's Engraved Business Card of Delacroix's 'Ice House Garden' on Broadway." *New York Historical Society Bulletin* 20 (October 1936): 110–12.

McLoughlin, William G. "Trade Cards." *American Heritage* 18 (February 1967): 48–63.

Means, Mary Elizabeth. "Early American Trade Cards." M.A. thesis, Winterthur Program, Winterthur, Del., 1958.

Metropolitan Museum of Art, New York. *Directory of the J. R. Burdick Collection.* New York, n.d.

Moore, Mary F. *Advertising Cards of the Eighties in Upstate New York.* Northampton, Mass., 1947. Reprinted in *New York History* 30 (October 1949): 449–61.

Neal, Keith, and D. H. L. Back. *British Gunmakers: Their Trade Cards, Cases and Equipment, 1760–1860.* Warminster, 1980.

Pullar, Elizabeth. "Baking Soda Bonus Cards: Arm and Hammer Trade Cards designed by L. A. Fuertes." *Antiques Journal* 35 (January 1980): 36–38.

Reif, Rita. "The Brisk Trade in Old Trade Cards." *New York Times,* 18 February 1979.

Shilton, Dorothy O., and Richard Holworthy. "Old London Bill-Headings." *Connoisseur* 66 (August 1923): 205–14.

"The Advertising Card Business." *The Paper World* 10 (May 1885): 4–5.

"They Called It the Card Craze." *Saturday Evening Post* 218 (16 March 1946): 28–29.

Winslow, David C. "Trade Cards, Catalogues, and Invoice Heads." *Pennsylvania Folklife* 19 (Spring 1970): 16–23.

3. HISTORICAL BACKGROUND

Adams, Samuel Hopkins. "The Great American Fraud." *Colliers Illustrated Weekly,* 7 October 1905.

"Advertising in the Drug Business." *Scientific American* 73 (5 October 1895): 214.

Allen, Charles Dexter. *American Book-Plates, a Guide to their Study with Examples.* New York, 1894.

The American Advertiser; Designed for the Cards and the Advertisements of Mercantile and Manufacturing Establishments. New York, 1850.

The American Advertising Directory for Manufacturers and Dealers in American Goods for 1831. New York, 1831.

"Art and Advertising." *Nation* 20 (20 May 1875): 342–43.

Atherton, Lewis E. "Early Western Mercantile Advertising." *Bulletin of the Business Historical Society* 12 (1938): 52–57.

———. *The Frontier Merchant in Mid-America.* Columbia, Missouri, 1971.

———. *Main Street on the Middle Border.* Bloomington, Indiana, 1954.

Ayer, Francis Wayland. "Advertising in America." In *One Hundred Years of American Commerce,* ed. Chauncey Depew. New York, 1895.

Babcock, W. H. "The Future of Invention." *Atlantic Monthly* 44 (August 1879): 137–46.

Barger, Harold. *Distribution's Place in the American Economy since 1869.* Princeton, N.J., 1955.

Bates, Charles A. *Good Advertising.* New York, 1896.

Beecher, Catherine E., and Harriet Beecher Stowe. *The American Woman's Home; or, Principles of Domestic Science.* New York, 1871.

Berkhofer, Robert F. *The White Man's Indian: Images of the American Indian from Columbus to the Present.* New York, 1978.

Bogart, Ernest L., and Kemmerer, Donald L. *Economic History of the American People.* New York, 1942.

Boorstin, Daniel. *The Americans: The Democratic Experience.* New York, 1973.

Brigham, Clarence. *Paul Revere's Engravings.* New York, 1969.

Buday, George. *The History of the Christmas Card.* London, 1954.

Burgess, Frederick W. *Old Prints and Engravings.* New York, 1937.

Burton, Jean. *Lydia Pinkham Is Her Name.* New York, 1949.

Butterworth, Benjamin. *The Growth of Industrial Art.* Washington, D.C., 1892.

Byrn, Edward W. "The Progress of Invention during the Past Fifty Years." *Scientific American* 75 (25 July 1896): 82–83.

———. *The Progress of Invention in the Nineteenth Century.* New York, 1900.

Carson, Gerald. "Early Days in the Breakfast Food Industry." *Advertising and Selling,* September 1945, 35–36, 66, 70, 74, 76, 78, 82; October 1945, 45–46, 78, 82, 84, 86, 88.

———. *One for a Man, Two for a Horse: A Pictorial History, Grave and Comic, of Patent Medicines.* Garden City, N.Y., 1961.

———. *The Old Country Store.* New York, 1954.

Chandler, Alfred D., Jr. *The Visible Hand: The Managerial Revolution in American Business.* Cambridge, Mass., 1977.

Chippendale, Thomas. *The Gentleman and Cabinet-Maker's Director.* London, 1762.

Clark, Thomas D. "The Country Store in American Social History." *Ohio State Archeological and Historical Quarterly* 60 (April 1951): 126–44.

———. *Pills, Petticoats and Plows: The Southern Country Store.* Norman, Oklahoma, 1964.

Clinton, Katherine B. "The New West: Themes in Nineteenth-Century Urban Promotion, 1815–1880." *Missouri Historical Society Bulletin* 30 (January 1974): 75–88.

Cochran, Thomas, and William Miller. *The Age of Enterprise.* New York, 1961.

Cohn, Martin. "Three-Color Process: Its History and Adaptability to Printing Methods." *Penrose Annual* 2 (1896): 33–35.

Coolsen, Frank. "Pioneers in the Development of Advertising." *Journal of Marketing* 12 (July 1947): 80–86.

Cooper, Grace R. *The Invention of the Sewing Machine.* Washington, D.C., 1968.

Crow, Carl. *The Great American Consumer.* New York,

1943.

Davis, Alec. *Package and Print: The Development of Container and Label Design.* London, 1968.

Diamond, Sigmund, ed. *The Nation Transformed: The Creation of an Industrial Society.* New York, 1963.

Dolmetsch, Joan, ed. *Eighteenth-Century Prints in Colonial America: To Educate and Decorate.* Charlottesville, Va., 1979.

Dow, George Francis. *The Arts and Crafts of New England, 1704–1775.* Topsfield, Mass., 1927.

Drepperd, Carl William. *Early American Advertising Art, a Collection of Wood Cut and Stereotype Illustrations used in American Newspapers, Almanacs, and Magazine Advertising, 1750–1850.* New York, 1945.

Dudden, Faye. *Serving Women: Household Service in Nineteenth-Century America.* Middletown, Conn., 1983.

Emmet, Boris, and John E. Jeuck. *Catalogues and Counters: A History of Sears, Roebuck and Company.* Chicago, 1950.

Fleming, E. McClung. "Symbols of the United States: From Indian Queen to Uncle Sam." In *Frontiers of American Culture,* ed. Ray B. Browne. West Lafayette, Ind., 1968.

Fowler, Nathaniel C., Jr. *Fowler's Publicity: An Encyclopedia of Advertising and Printing and All That Pertains to the Public-Seeing Side of Business.* New York, 1897.

Freeman, Larry. *Louis Prang: Color Lithographer.* Watkins Glen, N.Y., 1971.

Fuller, Wayne. *RFD: The Changing Face of Rural America.* Bloomington, Ind., 1964.

Garraty, John. *The New Commonwealth: 1877–1890.* New York, 1968.

Gentleman, David. *Design in Miniature.* New York, 1972.

Ginger, Ray. *Age of Excess: The United States from 1877 to 1914.* New York, 1965.

Gowans, Alan. *Learning to See: Historical Perspectives on Modern Popular Commercial Arts.* Bowling Green, Ohio, 1981.

Grand-Carteret, John. *Vieux Papiers-Vieilles Images.* Paris, 1896.

Green, Harvey. *The Light of the Home: An Intimate View of the Lives of Women in Victorian America.* New York, 1983.

Grego, Joseph. "Artistic Advertisements in the Eighteenth Century." *Connoisseur* 2 (February 1902): 86–93.

Habakkuk, H. J. *American and British Technology in the Nineteenth Century.* Cambridge, England, 1962.

Haller, John S., and Haller, Robin M. *The Physician and Sexuality in Victorian America.* Urbana, Ill., 1974.

Hampe, Edward C., and Wittenberg, Merle. *The Lifeline of America: The Development of the Food Industry.* New York, 1964.

Heslin, James J. "Bella C. Landauer." In *Keepers of the Past,* ed. Clifford Lord. Chapel Hill, N.C., 1965.

Hitchings, Sinclair. "Graphic Arts in Colonial New England." In *Prints in and of America to 1850,* ed. John D. Morse. Winterthur, Del., 1970.

"Home, and the Sewing Machine." *National Magazine* 12 (June 1858): 539–44.

Hornung, Clarence P. *Handbook of Early Advertising Art, Mainly from American Sources.* 2 vols. New York, 1956.

———. *Two Hundred Years of American Graphic Art.* New York, 1976.

Hughes, Thomas P., ed. *Changing Attitudes Toward American Technology.* New York, 1975.

Humbert, Claude. *Label Design.* Fribourg, Switzerland, 1972.

Huntley, Edward L. *Huntley's Ready Advertiser.* Chicago, 1887.

"I. N." "Machinery." *The Nation* 23 (November 1876): 283–84.

Inge, Thomas. *Handbook of Popular Culture.* 3 vols. Westport, Conn., 1982.

Jenkins, Macgregor. "Human Nature and Advertising." *The Atlantic Monthly* 94 (September 1904): 393–401.

Johnson, Laurence. *Over the Counter and on the Shelf: Country Storekeeping in America, 1620–1920.* Rutland, Vt., 1961.

Kaempffert, Waldemar, ed. *Popular History of American Invention.* 2 vols. New York, 1924.

Kasson, John. *Civilizing the Machine: Technology and Republican Values in America, 1776–1900.* New York, 1976.

Katzman, David M. *Seven Days a Week: Women and Domestic Service in Industrializing America.* New York, 1978.

Kirkland, Edward. *Industry Comes of Age: Business, Labor, and Public Policy, 1860–1897.* Chicago, 1961.

Kouwenhoven, John A. *The Columbia Historical Portrait of New York.* New York, 1972.

LaFeber, Walter. *The New Empire: An Interpretation of American Expansion, 1860–1898.* Ithaca, N.Y., 1963.

Landauer, Bella C. "Collecting and Recollecting." *New York Historical Society Bulletin* 43 (July 1959): 335–49.

———. "Literary Allusions in American Advertising as Sources of Social History." *New York Historical Society Bulletin* 31 (July 1947): 148–59.

Latimer, Henry C. "History of the Lithographic Industry." In *Seventy-five Years of Lithography,* ed. Patricia Donnelly. (Special issue of *Lithographers Journal,* September 1957.)

Lee, Ruth Webb. *A History of Valentines.* New York, 1952.

Lewis, John. *Printed Ephemera: the Changing Uses of Type and Letterforms in English and American Printing.* New York, 1962.

Lynes, Russell. *The Domesticated Americans.* New York, 1963.

Maillard, Leon. *Les Menus et Programmes Illustrés, Invitations-Billets de Faire Part, Cartes d'Adresse, Petites Estampes du XVIIe Siecle jusqu'a Nos Jours.* Paris, 1898.

Maindron, Ernest. *Les Programmes Illustrés des Theâtres et des Cafes-Concerts, Menus, Cartes d'Invitation, Petites Estampes, etc.* Paris, 1897.

Marzio, Peter C. "American Lithographic Technology." In *Prints in and of America to 1850,* ed. John D. Morse. Winterthur, Del., 1970.

———. "The Democratic Art of Chromolithography in America: An Overview." In *Art and Commerce: American Prints of the Nineteenth Century.* Museum of Fine Arts, Boston, 1978.

———. *The Democratic Art: Pictures for a Nineteenth-Century America.* Boston, 1979.

Mayor, A Hyatt. *Popular Prints of the Americas.* New York, 1973.

McClinton, Katherine M. *The Chromolithographs of Louis Prang.* New York, 1973.

McCulloch, Lou W. *Paper Americana: A Collector's Guide.*

New York, 1980.

Merten, John W. "Stone by Stone along a Hundred Years with the House of Strobridge." *Bulletin of the Historical and Philosophical Society of Ohio* 8 (January 1950): 3–48.

Miller, George, and Dorothy Miller. *Picture Postcards in the United States, 1893–1918.* New York, 1976.

Mott, Frank L. *History of American Magazines, 1865–1885.* 5 vols. Cambridge, Mass., 1938.

Murphy, John Allen. "Color That Injects Life into Sales Appeal of Mail Order Catalogues." *Printers' Ink* 102 (7 February 1918): 10–20, 25.

National Association of Employing Lithographers. *American Lithography; Its Growth; Its Development; Its Need of Tariff Protection.* Rochester, N.Y., 1909.

Nister, E. "New Patent Process for Mechanically Producing Chromolithographs in Three or More Printings." *Penrose Annual* 3 (1897): 105–7.

Palmer, H. J. "March of the Advertiser." *The Nineteenth Century* 41 (January 1897): 135–41.

Parry, Ellwood. *The Image of the Indian and the Black Man in American Art, 1590–1900.* New York, 1974.

Peirce, Josephine. *Fire on the Hearth: The Evolution and Romance of the Heating Stove.* Springfield, Mass., 1951.

Peters, Harry T. *America on Stone.* New York, 1931.

Pickard, Madge, and R. Carlyle Buley. *The Midwest Pioneer, His Ills, Cures, and Doctors.* Crawfordsville, Ind., 1945.

Pitz, Henry C. *Two Hundred Years of American Illustration.* New York, 1977.

Porzio, Domenico. *History of Lithography.* New York, 1983.

Potter, David. *People of Plenty: Economic Abundance and the American Character.* Chicago, 1954.

Prang, Louis, and Co. *Prang's Aids for Object Teaching, Trades and Occupations.* Boston, 1874.

Presbrey, Frank. *The History and Development of Advertising.* New York, 1929.

"Printers' Ink. Fifty Years, 1888–1939." *Printers' Ink* 184 (28 July 1938).

Pullar, Elizabeth. "Advertising Booklets for Children." *Antiques Journal* 32 (May 1977): 30–33, 35.

Pulos, Arthur J. *American Design Ethic: A History of Industrial Design to 1940.* Cambridge, Mass., 1983.

Rawls, Walton. *The Great Book of Currier and Ives America.* New York, 1979.

Rogin, Leo. *The Introduction of Farm Machinery in Its Relation to the Productivity of Labor in the Agriculture of the United States during the Nineteenth Century.* Berkeley (University of California Publications in Economics, vol. 9), 1931.

Rosenberg, Nathan. *Technology and American Economic Growth.* New York, 1972.

Rowell, George. *The Men Who Advertise. An Account of Successful Advertisers Together with Hints on the Method of Advertising.* New York, 1870.

Samson, Henry. *A History of Advertising from the Earliest Times.* London, 1874.

Schaefer, Herwin. *Nineteenth Century Modern: The Functional Tradition in Victorian Design.* New York, 1970.

Schlereth, Thomas J. *Material Culture Studies in America.* Nashville, 1982.

Scott, Kenneth. "Advertising Woodcuts in Colonial Newspapers." *Antiques* 67 (February 1955): 152–53.

Scott, Walter D. "The Psychology of Advertising." *Atlantic Monthly* 93 (January 1904): 29–36.

Seeger and Guernsey's Cyclopaedia of the Manufactures and Products of the United States. New York, 1892.

Shannon, Fred A. *The Centennial Years: A Political and Economic History of America from the Late 1870s to the Early 1890s.* Garden City, N.Y., 1969.

———. *The Farmer's Last Frontier: Agriculture, 1860–1897.* New York, 1968.

Sherman, Sidney A. "Advertising in the United States." *Publications of the American Statistical Association* 52 (December 1900): 1–44.

Smith, Henry Nash. *Virgin Land: The American West as Symbol and Myth.* Cambridge, Mass., 1970.

Sommerville, C. John. *The Rise and Fall of Childhood.* London, 1982.

Spitzer, Leo. "American Advertising Explained as Popular Art." In his *Essays on English and American Literature.* Princeton, N.J., 1962.

Staff, Frank. *The Picture Postcard and Its Origins.* London, 1979.

Stephens, Stephen DeWitt. *The Mavericks: American Engravers.* New Brunswick, N.J., 1950.

Strasser, Susan. *Never Done: A History of American Housework.* New York, 1982.

Takaki, Ronald T. *Iron Cages: Race and Culture in Nineteenth-Century America.* New York, 1979.

Trachtenberg, Alan. *The Incorporation of America: Culture and Society in the Gilded Age.* New York, 1982.

Twyman, Michael. *Printing 1770–1970: An Illustrated History of Its Development and Uses in England.* London, 1970.

"Uneeda Biscuit." *Modern Packaging* 22 (February 1949): 82–86, 172, 174, 176.

Wainwright, Nicholas. *Philadelphia in the Romantic Age of Lithography.* Philadelphia, 1958.

Washburn, Robert C. *The Life and Times of Lydia E. Pinkham.* New York, 1935.

Weibel, Kathryn. *Mirror, Mirror: Images of Women Reflected in Popular Culture.* Garden City, N.Y., 1977.

Weitenkampf, Frank. *American Graphic Art.* New York, 1912.

Wells, David A. *Recent Economic Changes in the United States.* New York, 1889.

Welter, Barbara. *Dimity Convictions: The American Woman in the Nineteenth Century.* Athens, Ohio, 1976.

Wiebe, Robert H. *The Search for Order, 1877–1920.* New York, 1967.

Wilmerding, John. *Important Information Inside: The Art of John F Peto and the Idea of Still-life Painting in Nineteenth Century America.* Washington, D.C., 1983.

Wilson, Charles R. "Racial Reservations: Indians and Blacks in American Magazines, 1865–1900." *Journal of Popular Culture* 10 (Summer 1976): 70–79.

Wilson's Business Directory of New York City, 1870.

Wishy, Bernard. *The Child and the Republic: The Dawn of Modern American Child Nurture.* Philadelphia, 1968.

Wood, James P. *The Story of Advertising.* New York, 1958.

Young, James H. *The Toadstool Millionaires.* Princeton, N.J., 1961.

Allan, J. N., 32
American Baking Powder, 62–63
American Cereal Company, 54
American Lithography Company, 67
American Machine Company, 89–90
American Tobacco Company, 41
Arbuckle Coffee Company, 93
Arlington Collar and Cuff Company, 61–62
Arm and Hammer Baking Soda, 56, 103
Ausable Horse Nail Company, 59
Ayer's Pills, 71–72
Babbitt's "1776" Soap Powder, 96
Balm of Gilead, 46
Barbour, William, and Sons, Thread Company, 48
Barry's Tricopherous Hair Tonic, 42–43
Basham, F., Modeller, 21
Bean and Brother Company, 71
Bell's Pond Lily Soap, 75
Belvedere Shirt Waists, 97–98
Bensdorp's Royal Dutch Cocoa, 101
Boell and Company, Lithographers, 73
Bonner and Company, Clothiers, 78–79
Bordman, John, Hatter and Furrier, 13
Boston One-Price Clothing House, 98
Bourquin, Frederick, 25
Bowen, Abel, 13, 20, 70
Bradley's Sea Fowl Guano, 59–60
Brainerd and Armstrong Thread Company, 65–66
Breck, William, Importer, 8–9
Brewster, J., Hat Maker, 14
Brott and Snow, Dry Goods, 15–16
Buckingham's Whisker Dye, 42–43
Buek, G. H., and Company, Lithographers, 97
Bufford Company, Lithographers, 69, 96
Bufford, John H., 20, 26–27, 33, 68
Cable Screw Wire Boots and Shoes, 77–78
Calvert Lithographing and Engraving Company, 41, 75
Celluloid Collars, 73–74
Centaur Liniments, 27, 29
Chamberlin's Concentrated Leaven, 26–27
Charter Oak Mowers, 81–82
Chippendale, Thomas, 6, 8, 10–11

Chorley, John, 14
Church and Company, 56, 103
Clark's Thread Company, 32–33, 38–39, 48–49
Clay and Company, Lithographers, 69
Clay and Richmond, Lithographers, 82
Clay, Cosack and Company, Lithographers, 31
Clee, R., 6–7
Coats, J. P., Thread Company, 48
Cole, Phineas, Manufacturer, 14
Colgate and Company, 76–77
Conqueror Wringers, 89–90
Coombs, William A., Milling Company, 55
Cosack and Company, Lithographers, 63, 80
Courier Lithograph Company, 44
Currier and Ives, 37–39, 48, 83
Currier, Nathaniel, 20, 26
Curtis, Cyrus, 100
Cushman's Menthol Inhaler, 90–91
Dando Printing and Publishing Company, 50
David's Prize Soap, 51
Davis' Indian Herb Remedy, 71
Dawkins, Henry, 9–10
Des Moines Incubator Company, 102
Dewing, Francis, 7
D'Oliveira and Company, 65
Domestic Sewing Machine Company, 50–51
Donaldson Brothers, Lithographers, 35–36, 56, 62, 67, 78, 81, 88–89
Dougherty, Alexander, Tailor, 17
Dr. and Madame Strong's Corsets, 86
Dr. Gutmann's Russian Vapor Baths, 21–22
Dr. Kilmer and Company Standard Herbal Remedies, 46–47
Dr. Kilmer's Female Remedy, 86–87
Dr. Price's Floral Riches Cologne, 91, 94
Dr. Radcliffe's Great Remedy, 40
Dr. Scott's Electrical Products, 47–48
Drs. Starkey and Palen's Compound Oxygen, 85
Dr. Warner's Perfection Waists, 95–97
Durand, Asher B., 14
Duval, Peter S., 24–25, 28
Edwards, John, Silk Dyer, 4–5
Electric Paste Stove Polish, 57–58

Empire Binders, 58–59
Engelmann, Godefroy, 25
Estey Organ Company, 58
Eureka Health Corset, 85
Evening Star Stoves, 56
Fairbank's Fairy Soap, 97
Farmer, Livermore and Company, 32
Fiske, L. I., and Company, 74
Fleischmann's Yeast, 79–80
Forbes Lithographic Manufacturing Company, 50, 54, 68, 77, 83, 94
Frowd, W., Boot and Shoe Maker, 16
Geer, Elihu, Printer, 19
Gies and Company, Lithographers, 75, 80
Gordon and Dilworth, 53–54
Gugler, H., and Sons, Lithographers, 83
Hamlin, William, 17–18
Hancock, Thomas, 7
Hansen's Dairyman's Products, 80
Harbeson, Benjamin, Coppersmith, 9
Hatch Company, Lithographers, 48
Hires Root Beer, 88, 92, 95
Hoe Company Printing Press, Machine and Saw Manufactury, 19
Hogarth, William, 6–7
Hooker, William, 12, 18–19
Hooper and Brother Looking Glass Warehouse, 20
Hopcraft and Company, Lithographers, 59
Hopkinson, Francis, 10
Horlick's Malted Milk, 95–96
Howe Sewing Machine Company, 34, 49
Hoyt's German Cologne, 92, 94
Hurd, Nathaniel, 8–9, 14
Imperial Granum, 55
Indian Queen Perfume, 71
Ivory Soap, 52, 99
Japanese Soap, 74–75
Jayne, David, 44–45
Jayne's Carminative Balsam, 76
Jayne's Expectorant, 43–44, 96
Jersey Coffee Company, 39
Johnson, Thomas, 7, 10
Jones, E., Lithographer, 21

Kakas, Edward, Furrier, 30
Karle and Company, Lithographers, 71
Kast, Philip Godfrid, Druggist, 8
Kearney and Childs, 20
Kendall Manufacturing Company, 52–53
Kimball, William S., and Company, 69
Knapp Company, Lithographers, 52, 91–92, 96
Knapp, Joseph, 21
Koellner, Augustus, 23–25
Lake Shore and Michigan Southern Railway, 31
Larkin, Ebenezer, Bookseller and Stationer, 11–12
Lautz Brothers, 52–53, 70
Lavine (Hartford Chemical Works), 94–96
Libby, McNeill and Libby Meat Products, 62–65, 72
Liebig's Extract of Beef, 103
McCormick Harvester Company, 80
McGary, Thomas, Painter and Glazier, 15
McLaughlin Coffee Company, 93
Madame Monand's Tan Remover, 42–43
Magnetized Food, 48, 91
Major and Knapp, Lithographers, 26–27, 55, 76
Malory, Eleazar, Joiner, 5
Mandery, Joseph J., Bicycle Dealer, 68
Marie Fontaine's Moth and Freckle Cure, 61, 63
Marks Adjustable Chair Company, 57–58
Marseilles White Soap, 52–53
Maverick, Peter, 14–15, 17–18
Maverick, Peter Rushton, 14
Maverick, Samuel, 15
Mayer, Julius, 28
Mayer, Merkel and Ottmann, Lithographers, 58, 62, 65–66
Mellin's Food, 54
Mensing and Stecher, Lithographers, 56, 96
Merchant's Gargling Oil, 44–45
Merrick Thread Company, 49–50, 66–67, 91
Milwaukee Harvester Company, 93, 95
Morgan, Enoch, and Sons, 52
Morgan, W. J., and Company, Lithographers, 51, 84
Mother Swan's Worm Syrup, 35–36
Mrs. Dinsmore's Cough and Croup Balsam, 87
Mrs. Holts Italian Ware House, 6
Mrs. Potts' Cold Handle Sad Irons, 35–36, 64, 73–74
Mrs. Winslow's Soothing Syrup, 45–46
Murphy Varnish Company, 31–32
Mustang Liniment, 44–45

Muzzy's Sun Gloss Starch, 38, 40, 66
National Association of Employing Lithographers, 102
National Biscuit Company, 99–100
Nelson, Morris and Company, 94, 96
New Home Sewing Machine Company, 50, 83–84
Newsam, Albert, 24
New York Advertising Sign Company, 34–35
Nigger Head Tobacco, 69–70
Norwegian Balm, 47
Old Dog Tray (Wellman and Dwire Tobacco Company), 41
Old Reliable Shuttler Wagons, 82–83
Ottmann, J., Lithographers, 45–46, 54, 86, 88, 93
Parisian Sauce, 65
Parker's Tonic, 46–47
Patten, Henry, Razormaker, 9
Pear's Soap, 52
Pendleton, John B., 20
Pendleton, William S., 20, 26
Pepys, Samuel, 4
Pinkham's Vegetable Compound, 45–46, 87, 100
Pole, Edward, Fishing Tackle Maker, 11
Prang, Louis, 1, 27–33, 36–38, 48, 103
Pratt, Charles, and Company, Refiners, 78–79
Presidential Suspender Company, 66–67
Prince Stetson and Company Tavern, 12
Quaker Oats, 54
Randolph, Benjamin, Cabinetmaker, 9–10
Rapid Transit Soap, 76–77
Revere, Paul, 8–10, 12, 14
Richmond Lithography Company, 55, 90
Rollinson, William, 16
Rosenthal, L. N., 28
Royal Baking Powder, 56
Sackett, Wilhelms and Betzig, Lithographers, 79
St. Louis Beef Canning Co., 69–70
St. Paul and Sioux City Railroad, 37
Sanford's Ginger, 68
Sapolio Cleanser, 52
Sarony and Major, Lithographers, 20–21
Sarony, Major and Knapp, Lithographers, 21–23
Sarony, Napoleon, 21
Schuessele, Christian, 25
Schumacher and Ettlinger, Lithographers, 44, 82
Schwartz's Toy Emporium, 93, 95
Scoles, John, 15–16

Scott's Emulsion, 91–92, 94–95, 97
Scourene, 88
Seiberling and Company, 58
Seibert, Jacob, Lithographer, 22
Senefelder, Alois, 20, 24–25
Sharp, William, 25
Shields, Charles, and Sons, Lithographers, 77
Shober and Carqueville, Lithographers, 37, 63, 65, 72
Siddall, Richard, Chemist, 6
Simmons, Abraham, 16
Singer Sewing Machine Company, 50, 91, 93
Smither, John, 9–10
Soapine Cleanser, 52–53, 56
Spalding Bicycle Company, 60
Stadler, Max, and Company, Clothiers, 69–70
Stimson's Sudsena, 52–53
Strobridge Lithographing Company, 102
Stull, D. C., Milliner, 30–31
Taylor and Company, Hatters, 61–62
Tew, David, 11
Tiller, Frederick, 17
Tiller, Robert, 17
Turner, James, 7–8
Uneeda Biscuit, 99–100
Victor Shade Rollers, 75
Vogel Brothers, Clothiers, 78
Waldo, Joseph and Daniel, Merchants, 7–8
Warner's Safe Yeast, 56, 96
Warren, C. C., Leathergoods, 38
Waterson, S., Drygoods, 38, 40
Welch, Joseph, Hardware Merchant, 8
Wells, E. S., and Company, 35
Wemple and Company, Lithographers, 69
Werner Company, Lithographers, 58
Wheeler and Wilson Sewing Machine Company, 50, 83
White Borax Soap, 74
Whitehead, Edmund, Butcher, 37
White Sewing Machine Company, 50–51
White Steamer Company, 81
Wilde, Oscar, 61, 63
Williams, B. S., and Company, Windmills, 83
Willimantic Thread Company, 48, 50, 77
Wilson, J. A., Meat Products, 64
Wrisley, Allen B., and Company, 74